Mira Dana was born in Israel to  origin. During her university ye army veterans and later in a psy drug addicts before taking her M chology. Now a psychotherapist apy Centre, which she joined in 1979, she coordinates the work on eating problems and runs groups, work-shops, training and supervision while personally work-ing most with compulsive eaters and bulimic women. She also lectures in the UK and Europe.

Marilyn Lawrence trained and worked as a psychiatric social worker before working with anorexic women in 1973 when she was employed by the National Health Service. She has also been a lecturer at the University of Bradford and co-founded the Anorexia Counselling Service in Leeds in 1977. She now works at the West London Institute of Higher Education and since 1981 has been closely associated with the work of the Wom-en's Therapy Centre. Her published works include *The Anorexic Experience* (The Women's Press, 1984) and *Fed Up and Hungry* (The Women's Press, 1987).

Also by Marilyn Lawrence

The Anorexic Experience
Fed Up and Hungry

MIRA DANA AND
MARILYN LAWRENCE

Women's Secret Disorder

A new understanding of Bulimia

GRAFTON BOOKS

A Division of the Collins Publishing Group

LONDON GLASGOW
TORONTO SYDNEY AUCKLAND

Grafton Books
A Division of the Collins Publishing Group
8 Grafton Street, London W1X 3LA

A Grafton Paperback Original 1988

ISBN 0-586-07429-5

Printed and bound in Great Britain by
Collins, Glasgow

Set in Sabon

To Our Parents

CONTENTS

ACKNOWLEDGEMENTS

There are many people who have helped us and without whom the book would not be what it is. The Women's Therapy Centre, where much of the work took place. In particular, the group supervision group, who took bulimia seriously and everyone in the eating problems supervision group. Susie Orbach for inspiration, friendship and encouragement. Marie Maguire, for her helpful comments on the text.

Marilyn would like to thank her mother, for unqualified practical support and interest over the years; Joseph Lawrence for his inimitable presence, tolerance and love; Geoffrey Pearson for his constant practical, emotional and intellectual support (especially when she fell out with her word processor). Thanks to her supervision group, for their dedication, insight and good humour; to Alexandra Fanning for her consistent wisdom and much else besides. A deeply felt personal thanks to Dana Birksted-Breen. Her friends, Hilary Graham, Bebe Speed and Lesley Day have provided that continuity of conversation of which books are made.

Mira would like to thank Jeanette and Rami, her parents, for their emotional support and for giving her so much unconditionally. She would particularly like to acknowledge the help of Liz Greene, who has had a great effect on her life. Of all her friends and colleagues at the Women's Therapy Centre she is specially grateful to her friend Sue Krzowski, whose calm interest and encouragement were such a treat; Shoshanna Simons for her passionate enthusiasm which never failed; Margaret Green for all those exciting conversations about therapy and politics and for her loving support and to Helen Davies for her encouragement. Teresa Hirsch, Birgitta Johanson and Katina Noble who in different ways were such helpful friends, both professionally and personally.

We would both like to thank Judith Kendra from Grafton Books for her enthusiasm and her sensitive contribution.

Our final thanks are due to all our clients, past and present, who have shared their lives so generously with us.

CHAPTER 1

Bulimia in Context

There is almost no one nowadays who has not heard of 'eating disorders'. Anorexia is much discussed and written about in the press; there is often speculation about whether one important woman or another might not be suffering from it. From pop singers to royal princesses, anorexia must surely be amongst the most fashionable problems women can develop! In the same way, compulsive eating is recognized as a symptom similar to other examples of compulsive behaviour, such as compulsive drinking or gambling. A variety of different types of group and club such as Weight Watchers or Overeaters Anonymous have sprung up in most major cities in the white world to try to force or cajole women to break their addictions to food. Yet while eating disorders receive so much attention, they are rarely properly understood. Why are 95% of anorexics women? Why are eating disorders so much more prevalent now than they were twenty years ago? And why do they only occur in certain parts of the world? These are the sort of questions which all too often are not asked.

*   *   *

The stories we tell in this book, the pain and distress which they reveal, do not make easy reading. They will often make the reader feel upset and appalled. They were not easy to write either. And yet it seems vital that if we are to find a more useful and positive way of responding to bulimic women, we must begin by telling the truth about the nature and extent of the problem. There really isn't any future in consoling ourselves with thoughts that things are better than they actually are, although we have all sometimes been tempted to mini-mize the seriousness, the anxiety, pain and shock which such symptoms involve.

This book, by two therapists with many years' experi-ence of working with these women, addresses itself to two different but connected sets of issues. The first is what causes individual women to develop such symp-toms? What goes wrong in their lives? How can they best be helped, and how can they help themselves? The second, and much more disturbing, is what does it say about the lives of all women that many who seem to 'cope' in fact deal with their distress in these agonizing and dangerous ways? What is this secret and inexpres-sible unhappiness which women seem to share and what is it about women's psychology which prevents unhap-piness and pain from being expressed in overt ways?

Over the years, we have come to realize that many women who do not develop the particular symptom of bulimia also recognize and share some of the central psychological features of it. In particular, many women have shared with us their own feelings of being 'bad' or perhaps 'mad' inside with only a façade of competence and normality. Again and again we have heard that the 'coping' which women prize so highly conceals feelings of neediness, chaos and self-doubt. Bulimia is not the only symptom which women develop as a response to these split-off feelings. Depression, anxiety attacks and the use of legal and illegal drugs are all consequences of the same social and psychological situation in which women find themselves. While we focus on the ways in which bulimic women dramatize their own internal worlds, we are actually engaged in an exploration of the inner worlds of contemporary women in a more general sense.

It would be comforting for us to be able to believe that this kind of eating problem, while afflicting and even ruining the lives of some women, is nonetheless very rare. This is what doctors and other health care professionals used to believe. This is what we all wanted to believe. Recently, however, it has become clear that eating followed by self-induced vomiting is actually very common – too common for comfort.

What is Bulimia?

In spite of all the interest in anorexia there is another, possibly much larger group of women who abuse food secretly and who have not attracted as much attention. They do not turn up at slimming clubs and obesity clinics, nor do they create shock waves of horror in their families and colleagues by their skeletal appearance. They do not usually become fat, nor do they lose weight dramatically. They do not often have breakdowns, and they very rarely ask for help with their problem. In recent years, their problem has become known as 'bulimia', 'bulimia nervosa' or 'bulimarexia'. What these strange-sounding words actually refer to is women who overeat and then make themselves sick.

Bulimic women sometimes also starve themselves for long periods of time and a few of them purge themselves with large doses of laxatives.

These symptoms can cause serious physical problems, such as damage to teeth by the action of gastric juices on the enamel, loss of hair, throat infections, throat haemorrhages and damage to vocal chords. We have also heard of women utterly depleting their bodies of essential nutrients, such as potassium, and experiencing faintness or even fits. The habitual use of large quantities of laxatives can cause even more serious problems.

The severity and frequency of the symptoms of bulimia vary a great deal. At one end of the bulimic continuum, we might find a few women (and perhaps men too) who regularly, but very infrequently, make themselves sick if they feel uncomfortably full after a very large meal. Although in contemporary Western society this is not a culturally sanctioned practice for relieving the discomfort associated with overeating – as it was, say, in the ancient Roman world – it is clear that some people nonetheless still use it. We also know that a number of women who follow rigid restrictive diets will occasionally make themselves sick if they are lured into 'temptation' by some food high in carbohydrate. Although we might find such self-punishment and self-denial sad, it is not for these women likely to represent a very serious problem in their lives and as long as it does not become a frequent means of coping with life, we would probably not want to label it as 'bulimia' thereby implying that it needs treatment. At the other end of the continuum, we have young women who have abandoned promising careers and who spend most of each day, every day, almost continuously overeating and making themselves sick until they finally fall asleep exhausted. For them, bulimia can become such an all-consuming preoccupation that we have known women who have sold their homes in order to have enough money to continue to 'satisfy' what can only seem like a hopeless addiction.

Most of the bulimic women we come across fall somewhere on the continuum in between these two extremes of the very occasional vomiter and the woman who has nothing else in her life but her bulimia. Although it is hard to generalize about the women who produce this kind of symptom, most, in our experience, are highly competent and successful at what they do. They tend to be copers; women who always manage to hold things together and get things done. Whether their work revolves around the home and meeting the complex and often conflicting needs of a family, or whether they are established in the world of work outside the home, women who become bulimic are really women whom most people would admire. We are not here talking about women who 'cope' in an aggressive or unpleasant way. Of the hundreds of bulimic women we have met, very few have been overpowering or difficult to be with. On the contrary; as well as being an impressively accomplished group, they tend to be responsive, caring and very good listeners.

Their symptom, often the only sign of distress and evidence that they do not really lead the charmed life they seem to portray, is a deeply hidden secret. Sometimes a domestic partner will be in on the secret, sometimes not. But certainly the world at large is never allowed to guess that anything at all is wrong. This means, of course, that the overeating and vomiting has been contained. The majority of the women we have talked with overeat and vomit in the evenings, managing during the day to carry on as though all is fine. Sometimes women can only cope with the day by eating an enormous breakfast and throwing that up. Again, sometimes women overeat and vomit at lunchtime. But it is always done in secret; we have never heard of anyone overeating in the office. After she has thrown up in the toilet, the bulimic woman will adjust her make-up and get on with her work – all smiles.

To most people, this behaviour, this overeating and vomiting simply seems incredible. Why on earth should anyone want to do it? Mania, schizophrenia, dementia – these are all forms of madness which are easier to understand. We can accept and feel sympathy for people who lose touch with reality and whose behaviour reflects their inability to deal with the world. But these women manage, on the whole, to cope with life. They are not mad. On the contrary, they are women who apart from their dreadful secret seem quite normal and acceptable to the world. Theirs is the kind of madness which elicits not sympathy, but anger from those who know about it. It is not the case that anorexia and bulimia are confined to middle-class young women. At the Women's Therapy Centre, we work with women from a variety of class and cultural backgrounds. Most of the Black and Asian women we work with were either born or brought up in Britain and although their conflicts and problems about being women are mediated through their own cultural experience, they are dealing with essentially the same issues as white women.

At ten o'clock on a Saturday morning, ten women meet together with a therapist in a room at the Women's Therapy Centre in London. They have never met before.

Most have never been to the Women's Therapy Centre or any other therapy centre before. They have registered and paid to come on what the Centre advertises as a 'bulimia workshop'. They vary in age from teens to fifties. One is from the Caribbean, another Indian, three are Jewish, the rest originate from various parts of Britain. None of them is overweight, several women are very slim. The therapist thinks what an attractive group of women they are. By 10.45, everyone has introduced herself and the group is beginning to talk about 'the problem'.

Sandra tells the group that she is an art therapist, the single parent of two small boys. On the days when she does not work, she gets the children's breakfast, takes them to school and returns home to overeat and make herself sick all day — sometimes ten times in the course of the day. By three o'clock she is exhausted. She cleans herself up ready to meet the children, cook for them, help them with homework, get them to bed . . . and then it all begins again.

Mandy is nineteen. She is preparing to take A-levels. She lives at home and describes her family as happy, loving and secure. At night she takes 120 laxatives before going to sleep. 'Not every night, though?' asks the therapist. Mandy looks down, ashamed. 'Well, usually. You see I feel terrible now if I don't.' Mandy begins to cry. She cries all day. Most of the time she is unable to speak. When she can, she says that nothing is wrong, she has no idea why she is so upset.

Gillian tells the group that at twenty-two she has no qualifications, eating disorders having dominated her life since she was fifteen. She is a beautiful, frail-looking young woman with blonde, pre-Raphaelite hair. She lives alone in a room. Most of her time she spends overeating and vomiting into a bucket. If she eats all the food and still does not feel satisfied, she will eat her vomit and vomit it again. At weekends she works in a pub to supplement her 'dole'. There she is attractive, hardworking and competent. No one there would ever suspect she was bulimic.

In fact one of the things Mandy and Gillian and Sandra have in common is that they have never told anyone before about their secret obsession. And so the day goes on. Increasingly, as time passes, women move on from their symptoms and begin to tell the stories of their lives.

Jacqueline was twenty-four when she came seeking help. She had had difficulties with food since she was twelve and had been overeating and making herself sick for eight years. She had married at the age of twenty. Her husband didn't know she had a problem until six months ago when she managed to confide in him. She works part time, and on the days when she is at home, she makes herself sick on average ten or eleven times a day. She is a very clever and beautiful young woman whom her friends admire and rely upon.

How can she confess to the people who know her and care about her that she does this awful 'thing'? She regards it as an activity which even animals should be ashamed of. It represents for her, and for many other people, the most sordid and degrading aspects of human nature. Jacqueline is not sordid. Her life is not degraded. On the contrary; to all external appearances, she has everything she could want. And yet she is bulimic.

Miriam is fifty-four. She has been married for thirty years and bulimic for fifteen of them. She has successfully helped her husband to expand his thriving business. Both her children have gained places at the 'better' universities. She is a lively, intelligent and active woman who has many interests outside the home. And yet she is bulimic.

Clare is a final year music student. Gifted as a pianist, she also won her first cello prize at the age of thirteen. Clare has 'good' weeks and 'bad' weeks. On good weeks, she attends every class, practises diligently, and maintains her reputation as an outstanding student who will have no trouble in finding work as a concert musician. On her bad weeks, Clare is not seen. She goes no further than the local parade of shops. Her face swollen and puffy from crying and being sick, she rushes blindly out to buy the food she craves. She spends all her days in the constant cycle of overeating and making herself sick. She collapses at night, exhausted, hoping that by tomorrow the demon will have departed and she can regain some peace.

These stories are no easier to listen to than the symptoms of bulimia. One of the women tells the group how she was sexually abused as an adolescent, another of how as a little girl she was mother to her younger brothers and sisters. The object of the group is to help individual women to focus on their own lives and difficulties, to share their stories with other women who will not be shocked or horrified and to begin to devise ways of supporting each other towards finding different ways of coping.

But by the end of the first day, the therapist goes away with a different thought at the forefront of her mind. 'What on earth is all this really about? What kind of world do we live in that women have to endure these terrifying problems in secret?'

* * *

It would be perfectly possible to believe that one or two crazy, disturbed women might develop the bizarre symptoms of bulimia. But what we have to confront are large numbers of desperate women, not at all crazy, from diverse backgrounds, outwardly competent and coping, whose lives are dominated by this terrifying obsession with food. Those women who daily request help with this problem only obscure the far greater number who are still concealing it.

We shall probably never know how many women suffer from this frightening and soul-destroying type of eating problem. It is not the kind of thing women talk about. Indeed it is normally the last thing they would ever dream of letting anyone know about. For every woman who asks for help with this problem, how many more do not? It is not like the other eating disorders. Its consequences do not show. Women who simply overeat often become fat. Their distress becomes visible. In the same way, anorexic women ultimately show their pain through their emaciated bodies and in their own way 'ask' for help. Far from bringing her to the attention of the helping agencies, the bulimic woman's symptoms serve to sustain her in the pattern of her life. But whenever this eating disorder is mentioned, or it receives any publicity, increasingly large numbers of these competent women come forward to confess the cost of their coping.

A magazine for young fashion-conscious women recently carried a small advertisement asking women with this type of eating problem to write in. They were amazed at the thousands of letters they received. At the Women's Therapy Centre, requests for help from women with this problem seem to be increasing all the time. Whenever bulimia is mentioned on the radio, or a magazine runs an article about it, whenever women begin to sense that they are not alone and that others too share this problem, then the requests for help flood in. Many bulimic women do not really acknowledge that their secret and shameful preoccupation is a problem until they see it pointed out as one. Many regard it simply as a dreadful moral failing, something which they might more readily confess to a priest than to a doctor.

A Short History of Bulimia

Until quite recently, bulimia was not recognized as a distinct problem or syndrome, different from both anorexia and compulsive eating. Hilde Bruch[1] in her classic textbook on eating disorders, published in 1974, makes little distinction between anorexic women who vomit and those who do not. She does not even mention the vast numbers of women who are not anorexic, who are not ill at all in any recognizable way, who nonetheless find their lives utterly dominated by the compulsion to overeat and vomit. This omission on her part is, of course, not at all surprising. She spent many years studying those young people with eating problems who were referred to specialist clinics. By definition, the women we are interested in, the ones with secret eating problems, will not show up in those settings. Until very recently, they have not appeared in anyone's statistics and so the myth persisted that they did not exist.

And yet those of us who were involved in working with women with eating problems *did* know about bulimia. In 1978, when we were involved in a voluntary counselling agency for anorexic women and their families, we would sometimes be approached in a timid, tentative way by women who were neither anorexic nor compulsive eaters (though they often had a history of anorexia) but whose main problem seemed to be a compulsion to overeat and vomit. We knew about these women, or at least a very few of them, but because they were never mentioned in the literature, because their problem didn't have a name, we didn't feel able to recognize them as a distinct category of women, with a different, though related, set of difficulties. Usually they were offered a place in groups with anorexics who were very thin and didn't vomit, and all too often they left, feeling yet again that they were the only women in the world with this problem and that their own needs were not at all understood. The only alternative was for them to join compulsive eating groups, where they were faced with both the envy of the compulsive eaters about their 'normal' or rather thin appearance and disgust and anger about how such thinness was achieved.

Not until 1979 did the first paper which talked specifically about 'bulimia nervosa' appear in a medical journal. Even then, the paper was subtitled, 'An Ominous Variant of Anorexia Nervosa',[2] thus still not really allowing the two problems to be separated.

What then, we might ask, really is the relationship between bulimia and the other eating disorders of anorexia and compulsive eating, and why has it been so difficult to recognize bulimia as a separate problem?

Bulimia: The Ugly Sister

If we think of the eating disorders of anorexia, bulimia and compulsive eating, we could understand anorexia as one extreme (abstinence from food, extreme weight loss), compulsive eating as the other (eating uncontrollably, weight gain), with bulimia somewhere in the middle: eating but vomiting, usually not much weight gain or loss.

In a sense, bulimia actually does contain distinct elements of the other two problems. Like the anorexic, the bulimic woman is terrified of becoming fat; like the compulsive eater, she is unable to control her eating. It is therefore quite easy to latch on to one or other aspect of the bulimic woman's behaviour, and define her either as a 'sort of anorexic' or instead as a 'sort of compulsive eater'. This approach fails to understand the vitally important point that the bulimic woman's behaviour – her taking in of food and then vomiting it out – can only properly be understood as one unified action. It is the taking in and then rejecting of food which is the meaningful element in bulimic behaviour and which singles bulimia out as entirely different from the other, seemingly related disorders.

The resistance to acknowledging bulimia as a problem distinct in itself has, however, a more insidious root. It is not always merely the result of confusion or misunderstanding. There is a real sense in which both anorexia and compulsive eating are easier symptoms for us to accept, symptoms which arouse more obvious sympathy and understanding than does bulimia.

Fat women, women who eat compulsively, although they are regarded as unattractive and 'weak-willed' are at least seen as honestly and straightforwardly weak. They may not be able to control themselves, and everybody can see it, but they at least bear the consequences of their weakness. There may be some feeling too that within such a big body resides a 'big' spirit or nature. We also have the popular mythology that fat women are 'cheerful', pleasant and good to be with, which makes them a group which, though despised in some ways, is well tolerated in others.

Towards anorexic women, our responses are almost a mirror image. Although their behaviour may be regarded as infuriating by those close to them, their ability to deny themselves and to control their bodies evokes an awesome regard in the spectator. Self-control is an attribute very highly prized in a society like ours where there are so many opportunities for over-indulgence and selfish decadence. Women especially are admired for their capacity to negate their own needs and keep themselves under control. Little wonder that beneath the irritation with anorexic women there lies an admiration of them, a feeling that somehow they hold a mysterious secret which enables them to manage on so little. The thinness of the anorexic is, of course, another reason why she is so envied by other women, many of whom are fighting their own battles with their own human nature.

So while the compulsive eater with her obvious 'weakness' both arouses our sympathy and makes us feel better about ourselves, and the anorexic evokes our wonder and admiration, what of the bulimic woman?

All the evidence suggests that professionals working with women with eating disorders share the same prejudices and myths about the problem as everyone else. Troy Cooper[3] has carefully documented the way in which doctors and researchers have reacted to bulimic women as though they were failed anorexics, utterly lacking in self-control and with little or no right to sympathy or attention. Unlike the anorexic woman, women with bulimia seem unable to manifest that mysterious control, unable to subdue their physical natures in the way which brings forth such admiration. On the contrary, their way of coping is regarded as disgusting and self-indulgent, repulsive and wasteful.

Bulimic women are often treated as frauds and deceivers. The compulsive eater who is unable to control her appetites is at least honest about it and becomes fat. The bulimic, on the other hand, secretly indulges her gluttony and then deceives the world by disposing of the consequences of her weakness. If she then has the effrontery to go to her doctor and complain about how terrible she feels, she is likely to get very short shrift indeed.

Another factor in the confusing relationship between the different eating disorders is that very often women who later become bulimic have had an anorexic phase earlier on in their development. Many of the women who seek help with their bulimia in their twenties had an anorexic breakdown in their teens from which they never properly recovered.

Our research indicates that a very common pattern is for a young woman to develop an acutely anorexic response to difficulties in her mid or late teens and to receive hospital in-patient treatment for this at the time. All too often, the treatment does no more than rectify the physical results of the problem without ever addressing the underlying psychological and emotional difficulties which brought about the anorexia in the first place. Thus the young woman ends up at a 'normal' weight, following the refeeding process to which she was subjected in hospital. However, she is still quite unable to accept herself at a normal weight and, following her release from hospital, becomes acutely depressed and often suicidal. Having had her rigid control of her eating forcibly removed before she was ready to attempt to nourish herself, such a woman typically finds that her eating becomes quite chaotic. Her loss of control terrifies her, and she discovers that by vomiting after she has eaten, she can at least control the consequences of her overeating. Such a woman, whose eating disorder goes, as it were, underground, is often regarded by both medical professionals and family as 'recovered'. A normal weight is maintained, a normal-seeming life again becomes possible. It is the cost of such normality which remains hidden and a source of such shame.

The fact that the bulimic woman does not appear to be in acute physical danger, that she manages to contain her distress within an ordinary life-style tends not to make doctors feel too worried about her. It is easy to regard her more as a nuisance than as a patient.

Why Now?

There can be little doubt that the numbers of bulimic women coming forward for help have increased dramatically in the past three or four years in Europe and North America. This, of course, is partly due to recent publicity about the disorder, and the recognition by some women that what they have regarded merely as a shameful piece of behaviour can be seen as a problem which may now receive a more sympathetic response. At the Women's Therapy Centre, there is a noticeable relationship between television programmes on bulimia or articles in popular magazines, and the numbers of referrals we receive. However, the increasing numbers of women with eating disorders in general and bulimia in particular cannot be solely ascribed to more women coming forward to talk about their problem. There seems to be agreement amongst specialists in the field that what we are seeing represents an actual increase in the numbers of women developing eating disorders.[4] But why? And why are eating disorders unknown in large areas of the world?

Eating disorders appear only to occur in societies where there is enough food to go round and where thinness is prized. While anorexia and bulimia are unknown in much of Africa and Asia, they are beginning to become recognized as problems in some of the oil-rich Gulf states.

It has been suggested that the increases in the incidence of anorexia and bulimia are related to the changing and conflicting roles of women in contemporary society.[5] Given that bulimia seems so clearly to be a symptom symbolizing conflict, this is a suggestion which has to be taken seriously. It is certainly true that in the past twenty years not only the roles of women but also the possibilities for women's lives have changed and expanded, so that while many women still occupy traditional roles within the home, many others are engaged in activities in the world either as well as or instead of what they do at home.

The link between anorexia and a high level of educational achievement has already been analysed in terms of the conflicts it generates for young women.[6] The bulimic women we see are a similar group to the anorexics but usually a few years further on. Often they are women who are trying hard, and successfully, to take control of their lives; women who want to make choices. They are very often caught in the conflict between the wish to be self-determining, powerful and autonomous and a need to remain 'feminine', which is interpreted as conciliatory, weak and dependent. This conflict is actually symbolized in the eating behaviour: the overeating symbolizes the woman's wish to be strong, powerful and her own person; her vomiting shows us the way she is pulled back towards emptiness, frailness and, of course, thinness. Most bulimic women can intellectually understand that they should not be judged nor judge themselves by something as traditional and superficial as their size and shape. But most also find such judgements irresistible.

This disjunction between what we intellectually 'know' and what we feel seems to us to be entirely understandable. It is the case that although women are now taken seriously as people in the world much more readily than was previously possible, they are also still judged to a very great extent by their looks and manner. Women politicians, for example, are still described in terms of their clothes, and are often vilified for not being sufficiently 'feminine' in their presentation of themselves. Women are still evaluated according to a double standard. It is towards this double standard that bulimia points us.

It is perhaps important to acknowledge that we do live in an age which seems particularly to value appearances. We are led to believe that satisfaction and fulfilment reside in a certain life-style and the acquisition of particular goods; that staying 'young and beautiful' is more important than what kinds of people we really are; that the part of us which we show to the world is more important than our private, inner selves. Bulimia is a symptom which puts outward appearance above everything. The bulimic woman will do anything with her distress, confusion, mess and upset; anything, that is, but let it show. We have come across women who over a span of years have become so desperate about their inability to control their 'shocking' and secret behaviour that they have made a number of suicide attempts and still have told no one the reason for their despair.

Bulimia is not merely an aid to slimming. One of the blocks to understanding its full significance and seriousness has been the tendency of the medical profession and of the media to regard it as such. 'The lengths some women will go to,' we sometimes hear, 'just to avoid an inch on their waistlines.' 'If they don't want to get fat, why don't they control themselves in the first place?'

While it is often the case that young women first 'discover' making themselves sick in an attempt to control their weight, those who get 'hooked' on it maintain the symptom for a variety of more profound reasons. For these women, being sick is not merely a means of controlling weight after overeating. One could equally well say that they overeat *in order to make themselves sick*. The truth is that we have to approach the problem of bulimia as a beast with two heads, never losing sight of the essential unity of the symptom. We need to be able to take it seriously as a symptom with a variety of meanings; it is not merely a bizarre or shocking piece of behaviour.

REFERENCES

1. Bruch, Hilde, *Eating Disorders*, Routledge & Kegan Paul, London, 1974.

2. Russell, G. F. M., 'Bulimia Nervosa: An Ominous Variant of Anorexia Nervosa', *Psychological Medicine*, 1979, 9, 429–48.
3. Cooper, Troy, 'Anorexia and Bulimia: The Political and the Personal', in Lawrence, M., *Fed Up and Hungry*, The Women's Press, London, 1987.
4. See, for example, Crisp, A. H., *Anorexia Nervosa: Let Me Be*, Academic Press, London, 1980, and Slade, R., *The Anorexia Nervosa Reference Book*, Harper & Row, London, 1984.
5. Orbach, Susie, *Hunger Strike*, Faber, London, 1986.
6. Lawrence, Marilyn, 'Education and Identity: Thoughts on the Social Origins of Anorexia', *Women's Studies International Forum*, 1984, vol 7, no 4, 201–9.

CHAPTER 2

A New Understanding of Bulimia

The approach to bulimia which is offered in this book is one which focuses on its underlying meanings. We have developed an orientation to eating problems in which we try to understand the particular difficulty which the woman has with food as a reflection and expression of difficulties she experiences in her life and in her inner world. This does not mean at all that we ignore symptoms; on the contrary, we see them as vital clues and links which can lead us to a more accurate understanding of how a woman understands herself and how her personal, inner world relates to the world of external reality.

Our understanding of women's symptoms and women's psychology suggests that eating disorders, and bulimia in particular, are accurate and meaningful ways which women use to express their distress and unhappiness. Our approach to treatment takes the symptom of bulimia as a metaphor or symbolic representation of the conflicts and difficulties which beset many women and which cannot find a more overt expression.

When we write about 'women's psychology' we are referring to women's experience in the world and in particular the experience of growing up as a girl and all that that entails. In addition, we are referring to how women internalize this experience. Our experiences early on in life do not, in our view, leave us untouched. Rather, they have a powerful effect in determining the way we feel and think about ourselves. It is the social stereotypes and attitudes towards women which, mediated through the experience of our own families, contribute to the way we think and feel about ourselves as women. These processes can also limit and define the ways in which women feel able to behave. Society has gone through a rapid period of change in its attitudes towards women, about what women are and what they can properly aspire to be. The result is that many of the social attitudes and roles which women learn are conflicting and contradictory. There are more opportunities for women and even pressures for women to be active in the world. Yet at the same time, we still have powerful feelings about the traditional role of women as wives and mothers with all that that implies.

In addition to the conflicting social demands on women, to which all women are subject in some way or another, each individual growing up has her own particular and unique experience of her own family. There can be little doubt that families vary in their capacity to help children develop a firm and positive self-image and to deal effectively with their own needs and the demands of the world outside.

In our view, the difficulties that women experience in such large numbers with food and eating are the result of both social processes and pressures *and* their particular experiences within the family. These two factors are, of course, linked. Families are part of the wider society and, to some extent, wittingly or unwittingly they transmit social values to their daughters and relate to them via social stereotypes.

In this book, we look in detail at both the social and family factors which contribute to the development of psychological difficulties in general and bulimia in particular. The important point is that we see eating disorders as the result of a number of different factors, some social, some individual. It is the very fact of the multi-causation which makes bulimia such a complex and addictive symptom.

Women's Problems

Eating disorders are particularly 'feminine' problems, not just because the vast majority of sufferers are women, but because they centre on one of women's most vital concerns, her body. Whenever we think about the psychological problems which women develop which centre on their bodies, we need to stop and think about the real relationship a woman in our culture has to her own body.

Women's bodies are *looked at*, by men, by other women and by ourselves. Perhaps the most important attribute for a woman to have is a body which is attractive and acceptable. But by thinking of and relating to our bodies as attributes, we somehow become cut off from them, as something which is rather separate from 'us' and which can be manipulated by us. This idea of being able to control and change our bodies is one which runs very deep in our culture and in others throughout history. Social stereotypes of the 'attractive' woman's body vary over time. The current social preference is for women who are very thin. Each year, it seems, there should be less and less of us to be seen. When we see 1950s movies of, say, Marilyn Monroe, an acclaimed beauty of her time, what we can now become uncomfortably aware of is a woman who is, by our present standards, overweight. Perhaps overweight is the wrong word. But certainly Monroe has the body of a mature woman, with breasts, hips and a roundness which is distinctively feminine. It seems that our present preferences are for women who are not quite so unequivocally female!

It has been suggested[1] that this rejection of the feminine reflects a profound fear of woman, both in terms of her new-found social power and with her more primitive associations of fertility and motherhood. This preference for women's bodies which do not remind us so sharply of femininity has a profound effect on girls growing up in contemporary society. At earlier and earlier ages, girls are attempting to take control of their maturing bodies, and to manipulate them into the kinds of shapes which are not in the least 'natural' for women. Bulimia is, of course, one of the ways which women might discover for controlling their bodies.

The Dilemma of Eve

This need for women to control their bodies has more than merely a cosmetic significance. Women's bodies have always been regarded as having contradictory and conflicting meanings. On the one hand, a woman's body is potentially a powerful attribute for her, something which will win her acclaim and favour. On the other hand, the female body is a source of shame, humiliation and potential evil. Woman is temptation, she is defilement, she is man's downfall. Yet at the same time, woman's body in her role as mother is the source of life and nurturance. She is seen and revered as the selfless, pure and perhaps asexual being towards whom all mankind should feel grateful and guilty.

Given the conflicting and contradictory meanings which women's bodies hold for us, it is hardly surprising that the body is often the arena within which women unconsciously choose to express the conflict which they feel in their lives.

If the body is the 'natural' arena in which women express their conflicts within contemporary Western culture, is it possible for us to say, in general terms, what these conflicts tend to be about? Most people who develop an eating disorder suffer from what we might call a low self-esteem. They tend to have profound self-doubts and feelings of inadequacy and unworthiness which are usually concealed and covered up. As so many of women's insecurities and self-doubts centre on the body, it is no surprise that many women develop an obsession with maintaining an 'ideal' size and shape.

Women and Food

In order to understand why so many women experience difficulties in their relation to food and why eating disorders are such common symptoms through which women express their distress, we have to look more closely at the rather problematic relationship which our society encourages women to have with food.

In most societies, including our own, women take primary responsibility for the provision of food. In very simple societies, where choice of food is limited, this may be a relatively straightforward role. In the Western world, however, many of us are literally spoilt for choice. This means that not only do women spend a good deal of time buying and preparing food for the family, but in addition they must decide and choose what to buy and cook.

Even women who are employed outside the home, if they have responsibility for a family, will spend a number of hours a week planning what the family will eat. Of course, we are not left alone in this task. The vast advertising industry, one of whose tasks is to sell more and more food, in increasingly complex guises, 'helps' women to decide what to buy, as does the medical and health establishment. The result is that we are bombarded from all directions with advice, suggestions and propaganda about food, most of it directed towards women.

This responsibility for family food brings with it conflicts and difficulties. How do women go about balancing the nutritional needs of the family with the constraints of the budget? Why is it that children always seem to crave those very foods which are least nutritious and most expensive? And who gets the blame if the Sunday joint isn't up to scratch or the children's teeth need too many fillings?

The provision of food and women's role as provider of food has a powerful symbolic as well as practical significance. The preparation and giving of food is one of the ways in which women show their love and concern for others in their lives. From our earliest years, women are socialized into nurturing, taking care of others. The ability to please and care for others is an important source of our self-esteem. It is hardly surprising then that women who have important and complex roles outside the family may hold on to the role of provider and nurturer within it and may still find themselves feeling guilty when the corn flakes run out.

In spite of their central role as providers of food, women are taught to be very cautious indeed in the way they eat it. The slimming industry makes an enormous fortune out of women's attempts to eat less and less and it isn't about to let us off the hook! Research indicates that the majority of women in our culture – between 80% and 90% – are what is known as restrictive eaters. This means that they deliberately try to keep their daily calorie intake to a minimum and do not allow themselves to eat as much as they need to stop themselves from being hungry.[2] In other words, most women are almost perpetually on diets of one sort or another. We can see most clearly the paradoxical and conflictual relationship women have with food by looking at the way food is featured in women's magazines. In nearly every issue, we find 'tempting recipes for 'the family' followed by hints on 'how to get into shape for summer', or Christmas or spring. This makes it quite clear that the delicious, attractive dishes which are featured are intended for women to cook for others but not for themselves.

The conclusion we are bound to draw from the evidence about women's dual preoccupation with providing food for others on the one hand and limiting their own food intake on the other is that the majority of women have an uneasy, and in many respects unhealthy, attitude to food. This does not mean, of course, that all women have serious eating disorders. What it does mean is that it is 'normal' for women to be caught in a conflict about food and eating and that this conflict has to do with meeting their own needs and those of others.

Women's Needs

It is certainly true to say that, in our society, women experience much more difficulty and conflict about meeting their needs and having their needs met than men do. Many women find it hard to ask for what they want, difficult to assert what they don't want and feel confused and guilty when they experience their own needs for care and nurturance. It has been suggested[3] that the nature of the mother/daughter relationship itself makes nurturing baby girls a much more difficult and conflictual task for mothers than caring for baby boys. The closer identification of the mother with the baby girl means that a girl is likely to stir up in her mother all the mother's unresolved conflict about her own needs and how or whether she gets them met. There is thus likely to be a certain withholding of care from girls which teaches them in a very direct way not to expect too much as women. In Chapter 5, we look at the nature of the mother/daughter relationship in more detail and consider its possible implications for individual women.

Eating as a Metaphor

The way in which a woman deals with her need for food, her pattern of eating, can be seen as a reflection of the way she deals with her other needs.

Eating, taking nourishment, is a fundamental human

concern. It is not, like breathing, a reflex action, and yet it is an activity in which we must all engage if we are to survive. As babies, we are entirely dependent on being fed by others. As adults, a wide range of social, cultural and symbolic meanings attach to the activity of eating. By observing people's eating habits, we can learn a great deal about their attitude towards themselves, towards others, their social world and their status within it. Eating is never a mere physical function; it contains and carries much more than is evident on the surface. This is why any disturbance in the eating function is bound to fascinate and appal us. The quite obsessive interest of the media, of literature and of the medical and helping professions can also be attributed to the fact that these symptoms are powerfully symbolic.

When we talk about a symbol or a metaphor, we have in mind a situation, an incident or a piece of behaviour which represents or correlates directly to another situation which has the same meaning. If we look at one, we can learn and understand more about the other. In the case of eating disorders, we can look at the actual behaviour and attempt to find the symbolic meaning of that behaviour which in turn will inform us about what is happening in a woman's inner world.

We can generalize by saying that a woman's eating pattern symbolizes that woman's capacity for self-nurturance, her capacity to take nurturing in and her ability to nurture others.

The woman who eats compulsively feels under pressure to take in everything; she cannot discriminate. She is aware that she needs something, that something is lacking, but instead of finding out what these needs are and attempting to meet them, she swamps herself with all sorts of things that she doesn't really need at all. She tries to limit herself, to ration herself, but she always ends up greedily gobbling up everything she can find. A woman who eats in a compulsive way is actually very bad at asking for appropriate things for herself. She may feel herself to be demanding, greedy and insatiable, but she usually ends up doing the nurturing rather than receiving it.

An anorexic woman, on the other hand, feels that she has to deny that she has any needs at all. Nothing can be taken in and there is little to give out. Or at least, this is what is being proclaimed by the symptom. Relationships are experienced as intrusive and dangerous. The only hope lies in self-sufficiency – a denial of any possibility of dependency or nurturance by self or others.

The woman who is bulimic, who eats quite large quantities of food and then makes herself sick, is using her symptom to say something rather different. Symbolically, she is able to take things in (unlike the anorexic woman). However, unlike the woman who eats compulsively, she is not able to hold on to it. What bulimic women can take in varies. Sometimes it is everything, without discrimination, sometimes it is more measured amounts. But whatever the quantity, once it has been taken in, it is no use. It is not experienced as nourishing, but rather as poisonous. It is not satisfaction but danger that the bulimic woman associates with her food. This is indicative of her inability to hold on to anything good, and not only at the level of food. Bulimic women often find it extremely difficult to allow themselves something which is good, such as a caring relationship, a compliment or some success at work.

Unlike the compulsive eater, the bulimic woman does not let it show that she is out of control. She passes as normal. Yet she always has the sense that her normality is a fraud and a sham. It is the hidden nature of the symptom which gives the first clues to what is being stated symbolically. The symptom says that although the woman appears to be attractive, well-organized and successful at what she does, she herself knows that really she is alone and starving. It may appear that she can deal with her needs openly and realistically, that she can express them and get them met. In fact, underneath it all, she feels like a greedy baby; her needs are too huge to be met, too destructive ever to allow other people to see. She cannot eat, but only, as she would call it, 'binge'. Bingeing is an important concept in our understanding of how the bulimic woman sees herself. 'Bingeing' is not eating. To binge is not to nourish oneself. On the contrary it is to make a mockery of the whole process of self-nourishment. Bingeing is 'sick' eating. And it is followed by quite literally being sick.

Unlike the anorexic, the woman whose symptom is bulimia is able to acknowledge that she has needs. They are not always suppressed or denied. But she perceives her own neediness as a great monstrous sickness, entirely out of keeping with the rest of her life. It begins to seem clear that for bulimic women, the throwing out part of the symptom, the vomiting, is just as important as the taking in. They are twin aspects of the same problem and if we are to understand the metaphor, we have to understand the symptom as a whole. This is what represents the woman's ambivalence about nourishing herself, finding a way of getting what she needs. When she takes in good things, she can only do so in a way which is violent and self-destructive. She takes things in in such a way that she is overcome by guilt and horror at her own neediness and can only find relief by giving up the nourishment and returning to a state of emptiness and isolation. The shame and agony involved in vomiting up the nourishment is a compensation, a suitable punishment for having greedily swallowed it in the first place. It is not just that too much food has been consumed and the fear of becoming fat makes vomiting inevitable. That is too simple an explanation. It is that needs have been perceived which are so terrifying that they must simultaneously be denied.

We can now look more closely at the actual behaviour of the bulimic woman and the contradiction it embodies. She consumes an enormous amount of food. She often eats whatever is in sight. She might eat raw food which should be cooked, frozen food without waiting for it to thaw, animals' food. She eats without any control over how much, what, where or when. Then she goes to the bathroom, locks herself in and in secret vomits it all up again, throws it all out. Then she cleans herself up, cleans up the mess and goes out relieved and empty of all the food and needs. Some women spend hours cleaning up after themselves so that others will not know about that secret messy part of them, that awful behaviour which occurs behind locked doors.

If we begin to translate some of this, and to look for the meaning of this symptom in the woman's inner world, we can see that the essence of the conflict is the good versus the bad inside herself. It is about having a clean, neat, good, un-needy appearance which conceals behind it a messy, needy, bad part, which must be hidden away.

REFERENCES

1. Chernin, K., *Womansize*, The Women's Press, London, 1983.
2. Button, E. J. and Whitehouse, A., 'Sub-clinical Anorexia Nervosa', *Psychological Medicine*, 1981, vol II, 509–16.
3. Eichenbaum, L. and Orbach, S., *Understanding Women*, Penguin, Harmondsworth, 1983.

CHAPTER 3

Patterns and Relationships: Bulimic Women's Lives

We begin this exploration of the lives of bulimic women and the kinds of relationships they set up with two basic assumptions which we hope will become clearer as the chapter progresses.

The first is that our relationship with our parents, especially the mother or care-taker, who is there from the start and for most people for much of the time thereafter, has a marked influence on our later relationships. The patterns we have experienced in early childhood become the patterns we expect from relationships; the way we were treated as children is how we believe we should be treated and deserve to be treated. We unconsciously choose people and patterns of relationships with whom and in which we can repeat our childhood experiences.

A well-documented example would be the woman who, as a child, was the victim of violence. She will often 'find' or 'choose' a man who is violent towards her in her adult life. Similarly, a woman who grew up in a family in which she was sexually abused may often find herself in later life in circumstances which are a repetition of the original traumatic event. The feelings and memories of childhood may have been repressed and forgotten, but the woman is compelled to create a situation in which these feelings are aroused again. This tendency to reproduce our earliest relationships cannot be taken as a sign that we have really come to like them. The woman who has early experiences of relationships in which she was abused and humiliated does not repeat them because she has come to 'like' being treated in that way. On the contrary. The compulsion to repeat is connected with a search for the familiar, the known, and also perhaps an attempt to recreate and then to put right the wrongs of the past.

The second assumption which we use in this chapter is that a woman's relationships to people and to food have something in common. Physical nourishment (food) and emotional nourishment (care, concern, love from other people) are seen as parallel. The way she eats, takes in food and digests it (or fails to) is similar to the way she takes in nourishment from her friends and her family.

These two assumptions are used to help us to understand how bulimic women relate to other people, what they expect from relationships, and how their lives feel. Generalizations are, of course, always difficult. There are, however, in our experience, a number of common patterns to be found in bulimic women's lives and relationships.

In order to give us a point of reference and to use a practical example as a starting point, here is a story told to us by a woman who approached us for help. She is a doctor, who at the time was working in the accident and emergency department of a busy London hospital. She describes a fairly typical day and in it we can see the place relationships have in her life.

Madelaine's Story

I feel exhausted. A long day at work has just about drained the last bit of energy from me. I was all right when I left home this morning. It's not an easy job. I feel sucked dry by them all – patients, nurses, technicians, doctors – they all want something from me. I feel like shouting at them all to get off my back!

But of course, I don't do that.

I nod and smile, and listen – and smile! and nod . . . and listen . . . I am actually very good at my job. But I get so tired, and I still have to listen to everyone. I feel as though I could burst.

Today, like any other day, I walk home from work. Like every other day, I feel agitated, tired and empty.

As I walk along the street, all I can think of is food. My mind goes blank, empty of all thoughts. Only three letters occupy the whole space – E A T – eat, eat, eat.

It's not that I don't think about food for the rest of the day. I think of it every minute, continuously, obsessively, like a bee buzzing inside my head. But this is different. Now I positively luxuriate in the knowledge that soon I will be home to my loyal, beloved, unfailing companion – food. Lots and lots of it. I begin to cut off from myself. It is no longer 'I' but 'she' who walks down the street. I am still walking, but I also begin to watch myself. I am two people: the person who does these things and my own observer. I watch her do what follows through a foggy curtain, like an image in a dream. I'd like to stop her, to ask her, 'Madelaine, what on earth are you doing? You are not even enjoying it. What has come over you?' And yet I can never get through to her. Whenever she is there, she is always in a panic, doing what she is compelled to do. I can only walk behind her and wonder what will come next. It has all happened so many times before. Yet each time I am stunned by the intensity, the urgency, the madness of it all.

The street seems darker. People disappear. I know they are still there, walking beside me, but I am blind. All I can see is the neon letters of the supermarket. In I go and grab a trolley. Off down the aisles. I do not have to choose what I buy as whatever I eat will find its way straight out again. It will all be thrown up, vomited away in no time. So I pile up the trolley and push my way to the till. I can't stand these queues. Why don't they have a checkout for each customer? These cashiers are so inefficient. Do all the housewives in London shop at this time in this store? Why on earth can't they let me through? Another minute of this waiting and I'll scream. At last it's my turn. I can feel how everyone is looking at me. I am sure they all know. I wish they'd stop watching me, judging me. Next time, when I'm in less of a hurry I'll complain about this cashier. Why do they employ such slow women? The bill comes to nearly £20. A bit more than yesterday. I pay in cash to save time, mumble something about shopping for a communal household and rush out with my huge bag, loaded to the top. I don't feel its weight, only the panic of my whole being to be alone in my own home and blindly and viciously to consume it all.

No, I can't wait. I stop at a street corner and thrust my hand down into the bag. Inside I feel something cold and wet in my hand. The plastic wrapping on chilled food. I tear it up. Can't see what it is. I reach inside and grab a handful of cold, wet, raw meat. I close my eyes and push it into my mouth. Not chewing, I swallow the small cut cubes of dead veal. Another handful. I can sense the cold smooth morsels slipping down into my stomach. I can move on now, a minute away from home. Find the key. Slam the door behind me. Into the kitchen. Throw the contents of my bag on to my big kitchen table. And I begin my celebration of despair. The phone rings. It rings again and again. My boyfriend. I said I'd be in. Why can't he leave me alone? Stop this ringing. I won't pick up the phone. Stop it.

Frozen cakes, frozen vegetables, raw vegetables, raw liver. I have no time to wait. No chewing. Just stuffing it down. Devouring. I am in my own dream world, my land of demons, where human niceties don't matter any more. Measurements and quantities don't exist ... where tasty, edible, forbidden and pleasurable have all lost their meanings. I am in the world of 'must', of compulsion, of drivenness.

I cannot believe my eyes. All the food on the table has vanished. Empty tins, bags and wrappers are the only evidence.

My stomach is bloated. The food is heavy and poisonous inside it. There is no more room to swallow. I pour myself a jug of water and force it down, glass after glass. I go upstairs. The dream has ended now. I weigh its consequences: five pounds of flesh on my already fat thighs. Agitated feelings start to come up. 'You did it again. Fourth time this week. You swore only at lunch time today that you'd never do it again. You foul disgusting creature.'

Upstairs, I lock the bathroom door behind me, run the hot water for a bath. I tie back my hair and put a bath cap on. By the toilet, I bend my knees. Face slightly over the white seat. Two fingers down my throat. I heave, breathe deep, tears in my eyes, and push my fingers in again, touching the back of my throat. Thank

God for the water. The food — warm, unchewed bits of green, red, orange, all colours — shoots out into the toilet. A few bits and pieces land on the floor. I must remember to clean that up. Tim might come round later . . .

Fingers in again, a whole stream of undigested food comes out. Again and again and again. At last I begin to see signs of the meat I ate right at the start. My stomach aches, my throat is sore, nose is running, tears in my eyes. My whole body feels tingly and aroused. I am in pain, exhausted. But relieved, empty and relaxed. While brushing my teeth, all the feelings I know so well flood over me; guilt, shame, disgust and self-loathing. I will *never* do it again!

But of course, she does. Over and over again.

In the course of this chapter we want to throw light on this seemingly bizarre episode in Madelaine's life and to use it to illustrate some of the important themes and issues in the lives and relationships of women who develop and use this particular symptom.

At the outset, we would want to draw attention to the urgency, compulsiveness and intensity of the episode, which seems to be so typical of the way bulimic women experience their symptoms. Madelaine makes it very clear that she desperately wants the food, yet knows that she will not really allow herself to have it. We can see clearly the dissonance between her respectable responsible job, and the way she experiences her self in her other 'life', in the bathroom. She needs to have everything nicely cleaned up before her boyfriend comes round. The woman he will later hold must be clean, happy and likeable — just like the doctor at the hospital; but of course, not real. During the bulimic episode, she needs her food more than she needs him. Food is actually the centre of her life, thought and action. It is all she can really trust. In her day-to-day life, she is constantly and continuously giving out to people who are troubled and in pain, who are needy and demanding. In her world, food seems to be her only trustworthy, consistent and soothing companion.

Needs and Fears

In this section we are using the work of the psychoanalyst Harry Guntrip, who wrote about people who have particular difficulties in making and sustaining relationships.[2] He suggests that it is not unusual to find an individual who is 'caught in a conflict between needs and fears which are equally intense'. This is a useful way of thinking about the bulimic woman's relationship to both food and people. In her relationship to food, by her consumption of enormous amounts, she is saying, 'I am desperately needy.' But later, by vomiting it all out, she says, 'I reject it all. I am terrified of actually having any of my needs met.' She shows a similar attitude in her relationships. She will often find herself 'driven into a relationship by her emotional needs and then driven out of it by her fear'. She feels too terrified to give herself fully, or, as one woman expressed it, 'to put all my eggs in one basket'.

Often bulimic women have several relationships at once, or perhaps none, while at the same time longing and yearning for an intimate relationship. She may find that her feelings constantly change, that although she longs for a close relationship with a particular person, as soon as they are available to her she has strong feelings of wanting to get away. Her fears of intimacy, of really being known by another person, can turn her good feelings into bad ones. It is like the food, which after it has been taken in, consumed, turns into poison, turns from something good and desirable into something bad and dangerous. In the same way, a close relationship and the possibility of real contact will turn from a very desirable fantasy, from something full of excitement, love and hope into something dangerous, terrifying, poisonous and hated.

In her fantasy, she looks forward to the day when she will be truly loved, when she will achieve the perfect relationship. Almost always, this fantasy is linked to the day when her bulimia will miraculously disappear. It will be a day when her life will fall into place, when she will be freed from that secretive prison she has put herself into. Deep inside, she feels that her needs are overwhelming and insatiable. So it is only in fantasy that these needs are ever going to be satisfied. She is caught between the terror of listening to her own needs, yearning for them to be met and the sense that she does not even deserve to have them, let alone have them met.

The problem is that her fantasy life and the reality of her life are a world apart. While she may derive a certain kind of satisfaction from the fantasy, she feels that it is her bulimia which prevents her from actually achieving it. The bulimia serves as a defence, a wall which prevents her from feeling what it means to be a human being in a frustrating world. In spite of her longing for everything to be perfect, the woman who suffers from bulimia often remains trapped in a bad or unsatisfying relationship. A good and loving relationship, though longed for, may be terrifying. She carries around an internal picture or image of herself which says, 'I am bad, needy, unacceptable and worthless.' A bad and rejecting relationship will reflect this image to her and hence will not create a contradiction between how she sees herself and how others treat her. A good relationship, on the other hand, will create a dissonance in her because it will continually challenge her feeling of being undeserving, worthless and unlovable.

The sense of not being able to take in anything good is combined with a sense of being bad inside, so that anything which is taken in is poisoned. This makes personal relationships very difficult to maintain. Loss of interest, fear, withdrawal, contempt and despising are all reactions emanating from this difficulty.

The dread of being smothered, taken over – in other words, losing the self in the relationship – alternates with the wish to devour, consume and have total control over the partner. Food then becomes a safe way of dealing with these two conflicting impulses; on the one hand eating, consuming big amounts, having complete control over the external 'object', while on the other hand vomiting, which is saying, 'I will not let this damage me or affect me or take me over. I will push it out before it can do so.'

With this yearning and terrifying dynamic, some bulimic women oscillate between being completely consumed with life and taken over in a manic way and withdrawing into total despair and desperation. Others find a way of avoiding these mood swings – perhaps because they are too exhausting – by taking a kind of middle position, by being unengaged, sitting on the fence, not letting life touch them. They will describe their lives as 'living through a curtain of fog', 'being in a world of dreams', or 'being surrounded by cotton wool'.

In our experience, bulimic women tend to have two possible ways of dealing with social relationships. Either she will have many friends and acquaintances, she will go out a lot, be popular, extrovert, someone on the social scene, or else she will have no friends at all, feel very isolated and lonely, believing that she can trust no one and that people do not like her.

These two ways of being in the world are not in fact so very different. The woman who is socially competent, popular and successful believes that she would not be so if people knew her 'real' self. The socially withdrawn woman is afraid to engage with people lest they discover how devouring and demanding she will really turn out to be.

The image she has of the two parts of herself is again very relevant. The part of herself which she represents by her behaviour in the locked bathroom, the part she feels is extremely dirty, disgusting and unacceptable, is completely hidden and withdrawn from the outside world. It is well defended, and no one is allowed to approach too near to it. The other, external, part which she presents to others is the part she uses to communicate with others. This part of her is still maintaining some contact at an emotional and intellectual level with the world and with other people. It cannot of course be fully involved with the world as it is always aware of the existence of a hidden, shameful, secretive part which can never be exposed or revealed. So any contact or engagement can only be partial. Hence the usual description a bulimic woman will give of herself as fraudulent, deceptive and empty.

The part of herself which struggles to keep in contact with the outside world has to be on guard continuously and prepared to defend itself on two fronts. It is aware of threats from the outside, and has to keep people at arm's length so that they do not come too near to the hidden untouchable part of herself. At the same time, this hidden internal part threatens to overwhelm, to take over even more of her, to take yet another part of her to become part of 'it', which she will have to hide, withdraw and cut off. This two-way defence system demands a great deal of energy, strength and the capacity for splitting or separating off parts from each other.

The part of herself she stays detached from, the part which represents needs, human feelings and dependency is also the part of the self which is able to indicate what it is that the self really needs, feels, wants, likes, dislikes, yearns for. She has no access to this part of herself, and instead she becomes dominated by a series of 'oughts', 'shoulds' and 'musts': a set of external rules which she has carried with her since childhood and which bear little or no relation to what she wants or likes. Thoughts replace feelings, oughts, shoulds and shouldn'ts replace real emotional or physical preferences. Routine, obsession and ritual serve the same purpose.

She will often feel confused about which needs really belong to whom. Often she will 'know' what other people want, but not herself. She will give to other people what she dare not experience as needing or wanting herself. She will let in people and experiences without any notion of what is good for *her*, but rather according to what she imagines they would like or want.

She will take care of others in the way she would have liked to have been cared for herself. She says 'no' to herself and more often than not 'yes' to other people.

The Fraud and Her Façade

This experience of two parts of herself creates a situation whereby the bulimic woman feels a fraud. This is a powerful dynamic which has a profound effect on her relationships to other people. Her sense is that the 'normal' presentable part of her is a façade, that she is only pretending that it is really herself. This is the part of her which engages with other people and believes that they would feel as rejecting of her hidden, messy, unacceptable part as she herself feels. She therefore feels as though she is engaging with other people on false pretences. In order to preserve the pretence, she has to be very appeasing, caring, understanding; a good little girl. On the other hand, she must not allow too much real intimacy to occur as this will bring the other person too close to the hidden part of her. There must be a point beyond which no one is allowed.

This means that people can be close to her — up to a point. A relationship is allowed so long as it doesn't cross that frontier or approach the forbidden territory. Anything or anyone which comes beyond that point has to be thrown out again — like the food.

The Secret

This feeling of being a fraud, of leading in some ways a double life, is what makes bulimia such a secretive symptom. The bulimic woman feels as though she has a shady secret which she must do all she can to protect. Over time, this secretiveness creates, or perhaps perpetuates, the inability to talk about the real feelings, real problems, real issues. Secretiveness and deception there-

fore become a part of all her relationships. We have
worked with women who have been married for twenty-
five years and bulimic for all of that time, and yet no
one around them knew anything about it. The whole
relationship with partner and with children is therefore
coloured by this secretiveness, by an aspect of themselves which women never share.

Having secrets can, of course, have a positive aspect.
Many of us like to have a part of ourselves which we
feel we do not have to share, something in our lives
which is only our own. This can be a source of strength
and power. In the case of the secret of bulimia, however,
the hidden and undisclosed aspect of the self is such a
painful and shameful one that the strength becomes fear
and the power isolation. The bulimic woman feels
trapped and imprisoned rather than having a choice
about disclosing or concealing the secret. Real communication therefore becomes very difficult.

Imagine having a habit that no one else knows about,
and which you feel is shameful and horrible. You believe
that if anyone did discover it, they would not want to
know you. You would then find yourself beginning to
behave in ways which would conceal the behaviour and
avoid giving any hint of its existence. You would begin
to hide the evidence, to lie about what you are doing
and to be continually on your guard. What that may
mean within a relationship with another person is that
the bulimic woman on the one hand denies major
aspects of her personality and her reality. On the other
hand a part of her is rigid and inflexible for fear of
being 'discovered'.

This creates a situation where the bulimic woman
becomes well defended but remains unprotected. What
we mean by this is that although she very strongly

defends her secret, her behaviour, her bulimia, she has no emotional tools to know what is good and pleasurable for her and what is dangerous and painful. She is not equipped, because of her very strong defence, to know how to avoid people and situations which very obviously contain danger, harm, destructiveness and pain. Quite the opposite in fact. She will be drawn much more to these than to those experiences which could nurture her and provide her with care. The feeling of having something bad, destructive and shameful inside her draws her to other people and situations which will confirm this view of herself. Often this reflects what she has learnt about herself and her relationships earlier in her life.

Often bulimic women will choose to have relationships with people who are for some reason unavailable. Sometimes the person will be unavailable in practical ways: a married man, someone who is leaving the country; or sometimes in emotional ways: someone who will hurt and deprive them of that nourishment and care they so yearn and long for but are terrified to take in when it is offered.

Control

An essential aspect of this dynamic is the bulimic woman's feeling of being out of control. Many of the women we work with talk of having a monster inside themselves which may erupt at any moment. The more you try to tame or repress this monster, the bigger, stronger and more frightening it becomes. The more secrets you have, the more secrets you have to create to cover the original secrets. The more control you may try to exercise over this 'monster' the more out of control you end up feeling.

In terms of her relationships there are two aspects to this issue of control. On the one hand, the woman herself keeps tight control over her feelings and emotions and herself 'erupts' only occasionally. On the other hand, she finds it very scary and unsettling not to have control over her environment and the people she relates to. To have to deal with other people's feelings who are close to her without being able to control them feels almost unbearable. She will oscillate between wanting absolute control over everything in the environment and giving up on control altogether. She will often have grown up in an environment which did not feel safe and which always left her with a feeling of chaos and danger. Now she has an internal sense of chaos and danger too, which only intensifies her desperate feelings of needing to be in control and the impossibilities of being so.

Her pattern of eating exactly parallels these needs and feelings. She eats in a chaotic and uncontrolled way, but then attempts to control both the food and the consequences of her eating by making herself sick.

Relationships: the Hope

The woman who develops the symptoms of bulimia has an attitude to herself which contains so much hate, loathing and contempt that she has no realistic picture of herself that she can hold on to. She has no acceptable view of herself as a whole with all her good and bad qualities, and no experience of herself as a lovable, valuable person. She is torn between an idealized view of how she should be and how she must present herself, and the 'real', unwanted, horrible self which she feels herself to be and which she must hide forever.

Her hope is that from a relationship she will get enough love, acceptance and understanding for her to be able to feel different and better about herself. Or perhaps that she will receive so much love and care, such a positive reflection of herself that it will cease to matter what she feels about herself. The fantasy is that she will be entirely enveloped within somebody else's positive, loving, accepting picture of her.

This means that she is forever searching for the other person who will mirror, reflect and validate her. She needs continuous reassurance, acknowledgement, love and compliments. The fact that she does not herself believe these makes no difference. In truth, even if this kind of total love and regard were available to her twenty-four hours a day, every day, her own self-image is so low that it would never feel enough.

This longing and searching for care and love and the disappointment involved in not getting it are often repeated from childhood right through to the present. This struggle for love is something which is going on inside her and which is externalized in her relationships. She may no longer be at all conscious of what she is yearning for, of what she is doing, but may only experience the sense of dissatisfaction with any relationship she finds herself in. She is often left with a powerful sense of not having got the love and acceptance she needed from her parents. She feels compelled to keep looking for it, repeating the search throughout her life. It is as though her parents promised her something which neither they nor anyone else is able to give her.

Being bulimic provides her with a way of avoiding

seeing and experiencing that yearning for love and approval and the emptiness and self-hatred perpetuated by the disappointment of not getting it. Overeating and vomiting fills up the empty space, while at the same time actively symbolizing how impossible she finds it to take in and keep in anything good. The bulimia soon becomes for her the excuse, her reason, for not being loved. 'How can anyone ever really care for me when I have such a terrible secret?' 'How will I win the respect I need when I do such disgusting things?'

Think of the image of the stormy sea: when the sea is calm and quiet, you can see the bottom, and all the details of what is there. On a stormy day only the waves are visible, the swirling of the water, but the details of what is underneath are lost. As long as she keeps the storm going by eating and vomiting every few hours (sometimes every hour), she provides for herself a sense of drama, a continuous storm. This keeps the emptiness, despair, anger and isolation well covered by the stormy water.

She needs her bulimia to help her to forget and deny her feelings of neediness, self-hate and unworthiness. She lives in the fantasy of finding the 'right' person, the person who will give her enough of the right kind of love, reassurance and respect so that things will change and she will no longer need to be bulimic. Both food and relationships hold out the promise of avoiding the pain and sense of rejection which she experiences. Food is the 'unfailing companion' to whom she can turn when disappointed with a relationship. But eventually she feels a good relationship will tear her away and free her from her obsession with it. She is trapped on a merry-go-round, but at all costs needs to avoid the pain of her own depression and sense of aloneness.

Abortion and Bulimia

Another issue or experience in a woman's life which we have found to be important and connected with bulimia in terms of its meaning and dynamic is abortion. We were first alerted to the possible importance of having an abortion by the large numbers of women coming to bulimia workshops and groups who had had one or more abortion and we began to think that perhaps women may use them to express the same conflicts.

There are a number of common themes in the experience of bulimia and abortion: both are ways in which a woman can use her body in order to express her unconscious conflicts; both also represent *incomplete* experiences. One could think of bulimia as the aborting of nourishment before it can be digested. One can clearly see that both bulimia and abortion are experiences made up of two halves, the first of which is deemed mistaken or bad (overeating, getting pregnant) and the second (the vomiting and abortion) is an attempt to redeem or get rid of the mistake. We need to consider both halves of the action together in order to understand the conflict which is being expressed, unconsciously.

Abortion is a one-off traumatic expression of conflict, while bulimia is a continually repeated acting out of it. But in many respects, similar conflicts are being expressed. Both actions are expressions of ambivalence, of wanting and not wanting. Both embody the hope (of nourishment, or new life), followed by the despair and giving up of what has been taken in. Both experiences carry with them enormous guilt, shame and pain. Of course, both bulimia and abortion have different meanings for every woman, but the women we have worked with have generally found it useful to consider the connections.

Bulimia as a Statement

Bulimia can also be understood as a powerful message within a relationship. Usually it is a message or statement which the woman cannot put into words. If she is going to give up her bulimia and find more overt and straightforward ways of expressing herself, it is very important that she comes to understand what kind of statement it is that the bulimia is making for her.

It is impossible to offer a generalized formula for the decoding of these bulimic messages, but in our experience they are usually the acting out of an angry, disappointed and frustrated response to something which is felt to be wrong or lacking in the relationship.

The bulimic teenager who experiences her parents' concern as intrusive and infantalizing might be using her bulimia to say, 'You don't give me what I really need. What you keep forcing on me makes me sick.' She cannot say this directly to her parents either for fear of their rejection, or because she feels they would not be able to withstand the direct statement. Instead, she develops a symptom which acts out the message.

The married woman with a family who develops a secret symptom of bulimia may be making a protest which for some reason she cannot make in words. 'You want to believe that everything in my life is all right, that you can give me everything I need. But there is a part of my life which you don't share which is tormented.' Again, 'I have to pretend to get everything I need from you. If you knew how terribly needy I really am, you would abandon me right away.'

Bulimia can thus be seen as a kind of silent, hidden protest about what is wrong with or is felt to be missing from a relationship.

REFERENCES

1. For a further discussion of this issue, see Norwood, R., *Women Who Love Too Much*, Arrow Books, London, 1985.
2. Guntrip, H., *Schizoid Phenomena, Object Relations and the Self*, The Hogarth Press, London, 1968.

CHAPTER 4

Eating:
Order and Disorder

The Regulation of Food

In order to understand the bulimic woman's preoccupations, to make sense of her behaviour, we have to ask several questions. Why is it food which she chooses in order to express her distress? What significance does food have which makes it such a powerful medium of expression? And what, specifically, is she trying to say by the way she uses food?

We want to suggest that bulimia is, amongst other things, a kind of perversion of what should be a natural function. That by her eating behaviour, the bulimic woman is expressing a powerful sense of things being turned upside down, reduced to chaos, and rendered dreadful and shameful.

Plato has some interesting thoughts about the significance of food and its regulation.[1]

The desires are ... those which bestir themselves in dreams, when the gentler part of the soul slumbers and the control of reason is withdrawn; then the wild beast in us, full-fed with meat or drink, becomes rampant and shakes off sleep to go in quest of what will gratify its own instincts. As you know, it will cast away all shame and prudence at such moments and stick at nothing. In phantasy it will not shrink from intercourse with a mother or anyone else, man, god or brute, or from forbidden food or any deed of blood. In a word, it will go to any length of shamelessness and folly.[1]

Here Plato is following the already familiar theme of the base, undisciplined and 'brutish' parts of human nature which lie beneath the civilized exterior and which, although innate, can sometimes still be got rid of. What we also find here is that Plato puts incest and murder on a par with eating 'forbidden' foods. It seems that the eating of certain kinds of food while abstaining from others is for Plato symbolic of the triumph of civilized human nature over savagery. He uses the term 'forbidden food' much in the way that we might use 'forbidden fruit', thus putting food transgressions exactly on a par with sexual ones.

The desire to regulate food intake in one way or another seems to be almost a hallmark of human civilization. We have not come across a single society of culture which does not or did not have rules prescribing how, when and what kind of food shall be consumed and by whom. Sometimes the rules have the force of law, such as the prohibition on alcohol in some Moslem countries; more often they carry the weight of religious authority, such as the food rules which go with caste in Indian society; at other times, as in our own society, they are merely strict conventions.

Prescriptions around the regulation of food fall roughly into four categories.

1. What counts as edible by a certain group and what doesn't.

2. How food is consumed, what conventions govern what we would normally think of as 'good manners' etc.
3. When and under what circumstances food is eaten.
4. What kinds of food are suitable/available to particular kinds of people.

We will go on later to discuss the ways in which bulimic women use their symptoms to override all four categories of food regulation. In order to properly understand the significance of this overturning of convention and regulation, we must first look a little more carefully at the importance of the food rules themselves.

The Edible and Inedible

There are very few absolutes when it comes to determining what can be eaten and what can't. It is probably true to say that almost all animal and vegetable products are eaten by some group of people somewhere in the world. Yet we all, within our own set of conventions about the edible, feel repulsed and horrified by what is considered fit food by people from other cultures.

The English, for example, have never really accepted snails as edible even though they are a considerable delicacy in other parts of Europe. Europeans and Americans generally dislike the idea of eating dog: on the other hand, the older generation of Chinese who enjoy dog would probably feel horrified at the idea of eating the little singing birds they so lovingly take for walks in their pretty cages. These little feathered creatures would be considered very fair game in Italy!

Similarly, we tend to have very strict social conventions about which foods should be cooked, and which can be eaten raw. In our own culture, although most fruits and some vegetables can be eaten raw, fish and meat only become 'food' when they are cooked. There are, of course, a few notable exceptions, such as the dish consisting of compressed raw minced beef, known as 'steak tartare', much prized in parts of Europe. It is probably not fare often served up within homes, but rather presents itself on restaurant menus where it attracts diners who are looking for an unusual experience! In fact, in our own society, the eating of raw meat is normally imbued with connotations of savagery or horror (the primitive 'cave man' or the werewolf). When we think about this in relation to the fashionable restaurants serving Beefsteak Tartare, we can see that it is precisely the juxtaposition of the civilized with the savage which makes the dish so enticing. If we are to eat, raw, food which is normally cooked, we do so under the most formal and highly ritualized of conditions.

A relative of one of us, now a man in his sixties, tells the story of how, as a young man, he courted a butcher's daughter – a beautiful girl, he says, with golden hair. One evening he called for her at her parents' home and she answered the door, according to his account, eating a piece of raw liver. He describes it vividly, across the years, the blood dribbling out of the corner of her mouth . . .

For him, that was enough, and he never called again! Any young woman who could eat raw meat – well, whatever else might she be capable of? This theme is exploited by the makers of horror films when they portray the brides of Dracula, beautiful and in a sense quite romantic stereotypes, but with a lust for blood.

The Raw and the Cooked

Anthropologists have suggested that different ways of dealing with food have a profound social significance for so-called primitive peoples. Levi-Strauss[2] for example looks at the way in which the cooking of food represents culture, the influence of the human group, whereas raw food is associated with being in a 'natural' or uncivilized state. A person who is thought to be naïve or unsophisticated – for example an unmarried person who has reached marriageable age – is made to eat salad. We often use the term 'in the raw' to mean naked, or speak of someone being 'raw', by which we mean uncultured. He further suggests that the practice of 'cooking' newly-delivered mothers (by covering them with warm clay) is a means of attempting to impose culture on a natural or 'raw' event and also a way of 'civilizing' the new-born.

We could summarize Levi-Strauss's view by saying that food is the link between the natural and the cultural. As human animals, we must partake of food (which is part of nature) in order to survive. But as human beings, our survival depends on the imposition of social categories upon nature. By means of cooking (which is the most direct way in which culture can transform nature) and other forms of social regulation of food and eating, the 'natural' is brought under the auspices of culture.

The accounts which bulimic women give of their episodes of overeating make it quite clear that they regularly eat food which is not normally thought to be edible. Raw meat and fish are very common foods for bulimic women to eat, as are vegetables like potatoes which would normally be cooked. Similarly, bulimic women have shared with us their accounts of eating tins of cat food or dog food, foods not generally thought of as being suitable for *human* consumption. Even more common in the experience of women we have worked with is the eating of frozen food. This is food which is suitable for eating, but not in its present form. Often frozen food will be bought especially for a binge, while it would be equally possible to buy unfrozen food. We also come across many examples of women eating quite unpalatable foods, such as flour, or large quantities of dry breakfast cereal. Such food can be considered edible, but barely so. It must actually be very difficult to eat.

It is a particularly powerful social convention that we do not eat food once it has been discarded or thrown away. A bulimic woman in an episode of overeating will often take food from the waste bin or the dustbin; such foods as fruit cores, vegetable peelings, or sometimes foods she has thrown away deliberately to stop herself from eating them.

Why We Eat What We Eat

When we look at what other societies consider to be edible and compare it with our own range of foods, it becomes clear that more is at stake here than just the taste and texture of the food. In some societies, food which others would deem quite acceptable is refused, even in times of famine, simply on the grounds that 'we don't eat that'! The idea of eating foods which are normally not considered edible brings with it a real horror, an automatic 'Ugh!' We can begin to understand more about the meanings of eating certain foods and refusing others if we look at cultures which, throughout history, have been particularly preoccupied with food prohibitions. Often, the prohibition on eating a certain food or foods is connected with an assertion of the autonomy of a social group, a sign of its distinctiveness. Within Judaism, for example, it is not that prohibited foods are considered inedible *per se*, it is rather that they must not be eaten by Jews. Jews know very well, and have always known, that some human beings eat foods forbidden to them. The point (or one of the points) of the prohibition is that Jews are not the same as everybody else. Similarly, English people know that the French eat snails and survive; the English 'Ugh, Snails!' is an assertion that the French do things that the English would not do!

The bulimic woman, when she ceases to discriminate between one food and another, when she blurs the boundaries between the edible and the inedible, is in effect saying that the normal mores of her social group no longer confine her. She will eat things which will produce a horrified reaction from her own kind. If the decision to eat one kind of food rather than another marks human beings out as civilized, asserts that we are not 'savage', then the bulimic woman is saying that no such thing is true of her. It is the uncivilized, the anti-social part of herself which she experiences as primitive and uncontainable, which is being expressed through her bulimia. Her eating of animals' foods, frozen foods and foods 'unfit for human consumption' are all indications of how she sees that part of herself.

To turn her back on the entire weight of social convention governing the regulation of what is considered fit food for humans is an expression of a profound sense of dislocation between the woman and other people. It also shows us the extent of her uncontrollable rage against not just individuals, but the human race altogether. And it is a symbol of profound despair.

Ways of Eating

In any culture where eating is defined as a social activity – in other words, where it is a *collective* activity – there are strict regulations about how it shall be done. So fundamental are these social regulations in our culture that children are taught before they can even speak what is considered acceptable in terms of 'table manners'. From the most basic rules, such as not speaking with a full mouth, and not putting elbows on the table, right through to which knife and fork to use with each particular course, the rules governing food intake are perhaps the most fundamental of all. In all human groups, individuals all adhere to the same set of rules which regulate eating; whether the chosen implement is a fork held in the right hand, or a leaf held in the left hand, we find that these norms are rigidly adhered to.

As well as dictating which implements shall be used for eating, societies carefully prescribe the circumstances of food intake. We do not eat standing up, but rather sit down, at a table, which is usually already laid with cutlery and condiments. If we are eating with other people we wait until everyone is assembled before anyone begins the meal. There might be certain rituals which mark the meal out as something other than a mere biological necessity, such as the saying of a prayer, or perhaps an expectation that people will talk to each other. This contrasts with the convention of the Ancient Romans of reclining on couches, or the Japanese custom of removing the shoes and sitting on the floor. There are clearly many possible ways of eating; the point is that each social group has its own established ways of doing it.

The woman with bulimic symptoms is quite clear that she respects none of the usual conventions about the ways we eat. She will not sit down, but will rather eat standing up or walking or running about the house or the streets. She never uses the appropriate implements. She will either use hands or else whichever implement – perhaps a spoon – will enable her to cram in the most food in the shortest possible time.

Any notion of 'table manners' is utterly absent. In fact for some bulimic women uncontrolled eating or 'binging' becomes a kind of bizarre mockery of a conventional meal. As one woman told us, 'When I binge, I do everything which would shock and disgust the people I ate with the night before. I eat with my hands, straight off the table – no plate, and I get food all over my face, even in my hair . . . It's like a kind of gastronomic black mass.'

Who Eats What and When

In some societies, such as that of the Ancient Egyptians, certain special foods are reserved only for the king. In totemic cultures, only the priest or elder may eat the totem animal which represents the group.

In contemporary Western society, we do not have quite such rigid prohibitions on certain people eating certain kinds of food, though it is the custom for some kinds of fish, such as caviare, and fungi like truffles to be eaten only by the rich or noble. In Britain it is also customary for certain kinds of game to be reserved for the aristocracy. The exclusivity of these foods is maintained partly by price and availability, but also by tradition. Caviare and venison are simply not part of the 'working class' concept of a diet, and one wonders whether lords and ladies have ever even tasted pie and peas or faggots and pease pudding.

We also have a particularly clear conception of what we regard as suitable food for children and adults. Fish fingers and 'alphabet' pasta are clearly marketed as 'children's foods', and certain desserts like rice pudding, jelly and ice cream all have connotations of childhood.

A meal, by most conventional standards, is a fairly orderly business. It has certain foods which are eaten at the beginning, it has main elements or courses which are followed by the less nutritionally vital aspects towards the end. We *never* reverse the order, even when whining children beseech us to let them have their dessert even though they haven't finished their main course! We also have foods which we do not actually eat at mealtimes, or if we do, only at the end and in small amounts – foods like chocolate, sweets or rare fruits.

The bulimic woman's binge respects none of these conventions. To begin with, she doesn't eat at mealtimes – or if she does, she eats in very restrained ways, not allowing her appetite to come into play. Her binge-feasts are always at other times, when everyone else has finished the meal, or perhaps while they sleep. She will eat and *mix* adults' food, children's food, meats and desserts. Her meal has no order, no rules, no pattern. Some women binge only on junk foods or foods which they consider to be unhealthy – foods like sugary cereals, processed foods, chocolate and ice cream. Dessert foods like tinned rice pudding, tinned custard and milk shakes are popular binge foods. Other women will alternate 'junk foods' with healthy things, like vegetables, usually eaten raw. The only rule is that there are no rules.

The Meanings of Food Regulation and Lack of Regulation

The regulation of food, the laying down of what we shall eat and what not eat, of how we eat, when we eat and with whom, this, as we have seen, is associated with the distinction between human beings and animals. For Plato, unbridled human appetite, not under the control of the higher desires, can produce nothing but terrifying chaos. For him, it seems to challenge the very basis on which civilization rests.

For Plato, the regulation of eating parallels the regulation of sexuality, and both are designed in some way to preserve the moral order and to safeguard the relationships of individuals to that moral order. Thus we can begin to see why the idea of a 'binge' resembles the idea of an 'orgy'. Both refer to the indulging of unbridled appetites, the one for food, the other for sex.[3] Both, too, contain the idea of perversion, the sense that something which should be socially regulated, done in the 'proper' way, is being used for something entirely different. Contained in both too is the idea that a function, a natural response of human beings which should be experienced as nourishing, positive, and self-affirming becomes instead a source of guilt and shame.

It is important to understand that rules and regulations governing eating are our attempts to impose order on the world. According to the anthropologist Mary

Douglas,[4] the food prohibitions to be found in Leviticus explicitly exclude and define as 'unclean' all animals which do not conform to the categories of nature recognized by people of the time. They are assertions that the world is not merely a chaotic place, full of an infinite variety of creatures, but that humankind can impose a set of meaningful categories upon all this.

In the same way, in modern times, our patterned and ordered ways of meeting our needs for food are our ways of showing that the world around us, and our own inner conceptual and instinctual worlds, are well-ordered places. The bulimic woman is contradicting these assertions. For her, all is chaos. And yet perhaps not quite. In as far as our rules and regulations governing eating constitute a kind of ritual around food, a ritual of order, then the behaviour of the bulimic woman, no less ritualized in its own way, solemnizes her commitment to disorder.

The Ritual of Disorder

Many women who develop bulimia or other disorders of eating express their symptoms in a rather ritualized way, always following the same procedures. Madelaine, in her story in Chapter 3, describes how she knows what will happen next. It is a pattern of eating which is repeated time after time. Often the woman feels as though the pattern must be repeated in exactly the same way. The cleaning up following an episode of overeating nearly always has a ritual quality to it and if she is interrupted in the process of vomiting or cleaning herself or her house up she feels filled with panic and despair.

What does the symptom mean for the woman? What

does her secret ritual of disorder tell us about herself? The disorder which is being acted out in this way is a demonstration of how her inner psychological world seems to her. In spite of appearances to the contrary, she is telling us and showing to herself that deep within herself, in a part of her which remains hidden, all is chaos and confusion. All categories and boundaries have broken down. One kind of thing spills over into another. Nothing is contained. She is revealing her own sense of something primitive, savage and uncivilized about her. But also, and more profoundly, her sense that something is deeply wrong with her, something which makes her defy all propriety and convention, and delight in turning everything upside down. Paradoxically, much as the bulimic woman loathes what she does, she also does delight in it. Her defiance of propriety and social order both expresses her anger and gives her a certain sense of power, however short-lived and unreal it might be.

Eating is such a basic 'natural' human function that to pervert and distort it in the ways in which bulimic women do has a highly dramatic quality. That is why it has such power to fascinate and appal us. In her secret 'life', her bathroom life behind a locked door, the bulimic woman acts out her hidden challenge and defiance not only to her family but to the regulation of conduct which lies, symbolically, near to the heart of the social group.

REFERENCES

1. Macdonald Cornford, Francis, *The Republic of Plato*, Oxford University Press, London, 1941.
2. Levi-Strauss, C., *The Raw and the Cooked*, Penguin, Harmondsworth, 1986.
3. Foucault makes the same point in his study of the prescribed regimen of the Greeks, in which food intake, exercise and sexual activity were all carefully regulated. Foucault, M., trans Robert Hurley, *The Use of Pleasure*, Viking, Harmondsworth, 1985.
4. Douglas, Mary, *Purity and Danger*, Routledge & Kegan Paul, London, 1966.

CHAPTER 5

The Childhood Origins of Bulimia

Whenever we come to think about a particular symptom, such as bulimia, and to relate it to a recognizable set of characteristics, we always want to ask ourselves, How did this woman end up feeling like this? What is it about her own background, her own experience of her family, which makes her express her unhappiness in this way? As psychotherapists working with women, we are suspicious of psychological theories which simply 'blame' families for problems. All too often, it is mothers who are being held responsible for everything that goes wrong in the family, or any unhappiness which befalls a member of the family. Our own understanding of families is that they are part of a wider society and to a large extent share and pass on the values of that society. 'Mother' and 'father' refer to socially constructed roles, not merely to the individuals who occupy those roles. But of course, the role is mediated through the individual, and the personality of the actual mother or father is very important too.

It is also important to understand that 'child-rearing ideologies' – the socially approved ways of bringing up babies and children – vary over time. While in the 1940s and 1950s it was thought important for babies to have a 'routine', with feeds at particular regular times, in the 1960s and 1970s it was considered 'correct' to feed the baby when she or he was hungry. Similarly, mothers were encouraged to bottlefeed in the 1940s and 1950s but 'breast is best' had become the slogan by 1970.

When we speak of the individual woman's experience of her family, of the earliest aspects of the mother/ daughter relationship, we are therefore referring to a complex mix of the prevailing beliefs – the kind of advice a mother would have been given by her midwife, paediatrician, health visitor – and her own unique personality and experience of her own family and mother.

In this chapter, we will consider the kinds of early experience which might be associated with bulimia. We are not necessarily stating that every woman who goes on to develop bulimia has a particular kind of experience in common, though certain experiences might be shared. Rather, we are suggesting that it might be useful to think of experiences in later life together with experiences in earlier life, since the one might throw some light upon the other.

In our work with bulimic women, we often find it useful to talk about the experiences of babies. This is not at all because we think of our clients as infants! Rather it is an offer to women of a way in which they might understand themselves better, another view of things which might be useful. Our experience is that many women do find such thinking useful. It can be a rich source of association and understanding which can help to ameliorate the very 'adult' and punitive judgements which women make of themselves. Symptoms which have to do with food, eating and the capacity for self-nurturance are always reminiscent of our early lives. This is because eating, taking in nourishment, is such a basic human activity. It is the first activity we have to engage in in order to survive. It is because of its very primitive nature, because it is one of our very first experiences, that eating has such powerful emotional associations for us all. In our earliest experiences, we are not able to nourish ourselves. Our ability to survive depends upon the relationship we have with our caregiver — or rather the relationship she has with us. Feeding is all about total dependency, and what experience we have of that state of affairs. The experience of feeding, and more importantly of being fed, is our earliest and perhaps our most profound experience of nurturance, of having our needs met or not met.

The psychoanalyst, Guntrip,[1] drawing on the work of W. R. D. Fairbairn, although he doesn't write specifically about the symptom of bulimia, clearly recognizes the personality constellation we have been describing, where there is such a marked degree of ambivalence about needs and neediness that the woman can never get what she really wants. He suggests that this dilemma can be understood in terms of the earliest relationships which the baby forms with its mother. He says, 'The situation which calls out the reaction is that of being faced with a desired but deserting object.' In adulthood, he suggests, '. . . This entire problem is frequently worked out over food. The person is hungry but rejects both food and people.' Faced with something which she longs for, but which she feels is unreliable, she first feels exaggeratedly hungry and then denies her hunger. She eats a great deal, but then vomits what she has eaten. The people she cannot possess, she cuts off from.

Symbolically, it is as though she wants to possess, consume and control the person she desires (ultimately representing the mother). Not being able to do so, she consumes the food instead. She then becomes so terrified of having admitted to her needs that she has to deny them immediately and throw up what she has just taken in. Her wish is to eat on and on endlessly, to get as much as she can inside her before it is taken away. Her attitude is *incorporative* in that her aim is to get something inside herself where she cannot be robbed of it; she has no confidence about being given enough.

Looking back to infancy again, we can see that 'the breast the baby is sure of can be sucked at contentedly and let go when she feels satisfied. The baby knows it will be available when she needs it again. The breast that does not come when it is needed is not satisfying even when the baby has it, because of the knowledge that it might be snatched away before the need is met.'[2]

This gives rise to a desperate hungry urge to make sure of the breast, not merely by sucking at it, but by *swallowing* it, thus getting it inside where it cannot be taken away. 'The impulse changes from taking in *from* the breast into an omnivorous urge to take in *the whole breast itself*.'[3] Guntrip sums it up by describing the different attitudes which babies might take up in terms of their earliest feelings connected with feeding: 'The contented baby sucks, the angry baby bites, the hungry baby wants to swallow.'

There are striking parallels here with the adult woman with bulimic symptoms who will often talk of her tremendous urge to consume or eat up other people.

According to Fairbairn, the problems for the hungry baby do not end here. The baby is faced with the situation that 'You can't eat your cake and have it.'[4]

This wish to devour, swallow up and incorporate leads to fears for the safety of the loved person. The anxiety is that the other person will be utterly consumed and devoured and will cease to exist as a source of love.

The terrible dilemma here is that she experiences her love itself as destructive and so she dares not love anyone. Instead she either withdraws into detachment and aloofness or else creates relationships where she herself becomes lost and swallowed up. All intimate relationships are experienced in terms of devouring and swallowing up and are too dangerous to be risked.

Her fear of the destructive quality of her own love makes the woman with this kind of problem tend to withdraw from people in the real world. She cuts off from her feelings and no longer feels much interest in others. However, in her inner world, her wish to devour and swallow up remains active. The secret symptom of bulimia may be her only link with it.

What this means for the woman is that she feels continually driven to act upon that oral-sadistic urge, and her symptom is actually the acting out of this urge. She is forced to gratify this drive secretly, as it is both repressed from consciousness and, as she experiences it, dangerous. By confining the part of herself which she experiences as destructive and terrifying to her inner, private world, she keeps everyone she comes into contact with safe from her devouring destructiveness. Everyone, that is, except herself. She confronts the shameful monster she wants to disown each time she overeats.

Since her basic problems in relation to other people are connected to her early relations to the breast, food and eating naturally play a large part in her struggle to solve these problems. Her reactions to food and to people are fundamentally the same. They both comprise a need to possess and incorporate, which is negated by a fear of taking in, accepting and devouring.

Mothers and Their Baby Daughters

What we have been describing here is a situation in which the baby is being deprived. Not *totally* deprived, not abandoned or abused or neglected in ways which would call forth sympathy from other adults. Indeed, the kind of relative deprivation we have been describing almost always goes unnoticed and unremarked.

Recent psychological studies of the relationships between mothers and baby daughters suggest that even under the most favourable of circumstances, mothers are likely to experience quite a lot of difficulty in meeting the needs of girls. Some writers would go so far as to suggest that it is *normal* in our society for baby girls to be given less than enough by their mothers.[5]

The difficulty for mothers in meeting the real needs of their baby daughters has at its origins the very fact that mother and daughter share a gender identity and so there is a much closer identification between the mother and her baby girl than her baby boy. The very fact that they are both female means that the mother is able to see herself and experience herself very much more through her daughter. Mothers often describe the way in which when they first see their baby daughters, they almost feel as though they were looking at themselves, whereas with a son, there is a clear recognition that he is different and someone whom the mother will have to get to know. The increased identification with the baby daughter immediately presents the mother with two special difficulties.

The first is her tendency to project on to the baby. The second is her unconscious repetition on this baby of her own deprivation. The tendency to project will make it difficult for the mother to be sure, when she tends to this baby, whether she is meeting the baby's needs or what she thinks of as the baby's needs. She may feel that with this girl, who is so much like herself, she has a special empathic understanding of what the baby needs and when: when she is hungry, when she's had enough; what at any precise moment her mood state might be. The fact is that as well as being a girl this baby is also a person with her own unique needs and feelings and so sometimes the mother's intuition will be right, but sometimes it will be wrong. There will be times when the baby's attempts to communicate to its mother what it needs will be lost because of the mother's belief that she really knows this child already and does not have to listen to it. The result is that the baby girl's needs will not be heard, responded to or met.

If we are right and mothers from one generation to another have difficulty in meeting the needs of their baby girls, then the new mother with her needy baby girl will see before her someone who reminds her painfully of herself and of all the needs she still has and which were never met for her by her mother. While the conscious part of the mother will want to do the best for her daughter and give her what she never had herself, the unconscious part – which is actually where the pain of all these unmet needs is located – will feel bitter and envious and unable to give her daughter what she never had herself. What she will do instead is to look after the baby girl well, to meet all her physical needs adequately, but never quite to give the baby the emotional responsiveness which she so much needs. The baby girl will be fed enough to keep her healthy, but never quite when she needs it, or quite as much as she might have wanted. When the mother thinks of her needy baby girl, she is confronted with the spectre of herself as a needy little girl, and the only way to deal with her own hurt and angry feelings is to make sure that her own little girl doesn't quite get enough either.

In addition to these emotional difficulties which the mother might have and which are connected to her own experiences of being nurtured, she also knows that as a woman her own baby, when she is grown up, will not be allowed to have her needs met. On the contrary, she knows from her own experience that her daughter's role as a woman will be to meet the needs of others. We can therefore see that within that earliest relationship with her mother, the little girl is being taught not to expect too much. At the same time as not giving her daughter quite enough of what she needs, the mother, because of her identification with her daughter, remains emotionally very close to her. This relative 'deprivation' is not experienced as a distancing by the mother but rather as a kind of withholding from within a very close relationship. If we think back now to Fairbairn's idea of the desired but deserting object, we can see how easy it might be for a baby girl to come to feel that her mother, her source of nurturance, is not fully available to her and never gives her quite what she needs.

We are not talking here of mothers who are themselves psychologically or emotionally ill, but rather about mothers who have grown up as women in a patriarchal culture and who are reproducing in their daughters all that it means to be a 'good' woman; a woman whose *own* needs are not allowed to dominate, who does not expect too much and who is able to find satisfaction by focusing on the needs of others. We are suggesting that what we have come to regard as the 'normal' mother/daughter relationship may contain within it certain elements which are destructive enough to lead to serious difficulties in the area of self-nurturance and meeting of need.[6] Some parents, of course, do have very much more serious problems themselves and when this is the case, it is often their daughters to whom these difficulties are passed on.

Alice Miller is a psychologist who writes about these disturbed parents.[7] She suggests that some parents, who have never been loved fully for themselves, offer their children love in a conditional or partial way: certain aspects of the baby are found lovable, whilst other parts of her are rejected. In order to keep the love of the parents, the child has to disown, to cut off parts of her own experience which are not accepted by the parents. Often, in order to maintain the parents' affection the child feels that she has to deny, cut off or get rid of any feelings of which the parents do not approve or which cause anxiety in the parents. A number of the bulimic women we have worked with have initially felt quite cut off from and unentitled to their own feelings. A little girl may have to repress all jealousy, for example, when a new baby is born. Her mother has never herself had her own jealous and destructive feelings tolerated and so cannot allow her daughter her own feelings. The daughter has to suppress and deny her own experience, her own reality, and develop instead a kind of false self where none of those feelings exist. She salvages her relationship with her parents, but at the cost of losing a part of herself. The feelings which are forbidden to the child usually represent a split-off and unintegrated part of one of the parents, which they themselves have always been terrified to acknowledge.

An example. A mother, who was an unwanted second daughter, was continually shamed and humiliated for being less attractive and less intelligent than her elder sister. In order to survive psychologically, this child ignored the abuse and insults from the mother and instead set out to please her and to placate the older sister. She became the perfect little girl, not like her arrogant sister, but always ready to help her mother to care for the family. When she had her own daughter, she of course cared for her very well – much better in fact than she herself was cared for. What she could not tolerate, however, were all the feelings she had had to suppress. Her own daughter was told that anger, resentment, envy, jealousy were all terrible feelings which she had no right to feel; after all hadn't she so much more to feel grateful for than her own poor mother? Thus any 'bad' feelings, or, rather, natural feelings of anger, envy or displeasure immediately made the little girl feel not only bad and unacceptable to her mother, but also guilty for making her mother suffer even more than she had already done. This mother, unlike her own mother, was able to give her daughter some good reflections of herself and her own identity, but only on condition that the child developed the false self which was compliant, helpful and always happy.

The daughter who grows up with a part of herself which she has to split off and deny is very vulnerable to a symptom like bulimia. The bulimia represents the split-off part, an aspect of herself which she doesn't really know, doesn't feel as part of herself, but which she is nonetheless ashamed of and which confirms to her that she isn't really the nice person which people believe her to be.

Alice Miller sums it up like this. 'As the child grows up, he cannot cease living his own truth, and expressing it somewhere, perhaps in complete secrecy. In this way a person can have adapted completely to the demands of his surroundings and can have developed a false self, but in his perversion or his obsessional neurosis he still allows a portion of his true self to survive – in torment.'[8]

In this instance, we are not talking about the development of a perversion, which might harm or frighten other people, or an obsessional neurosis, which might stop the woman from doing her job; here we are thinking of a much more feminine way of keeping alive a despised part of the self. The symptom of bulimia harms no one but the woman herself and enables her to keep up the pretence of coping.

Fathers and Daughters

So far we have been looking at the nature of the mother/daughter relationship. Our work suggests that the role played by the father in the girl's life also has an important place in the inner world of the bulimic woman.

Various writers have speculated about the role of fathers in the development of their daughters. It has often been conceptualized as the means by which the young child moves from the environment of the home and shifts its focus out to the wider world. This involves a shift from the milieu of the two-person relationship of child and mother to one in which relationships with others form a part. The father may well be the first such 'other'. It has been suggested that at adolescence the father is important to his daughter in that he can appreciate and confirm her attractiveness within the 'safe' confines of the family, her sexuality being protected and cared for within the security provided by the incest taboo. The father also provides, by his close involvement with the mother, a helpful degree of separation between mother and daughter.

D. W. Winnicott suggests that in the early months of life, the father's chief role lies in supporting the mother, both economically and emotionally, so that she can devote her time to the baby.[9] Andrew Samuels in his book, *The Father*,[10] suggests that the father may be recognized by the infant as early as four or five months. This means that the father can play a part in the vital process of mirroring or reflecting the baby to itself which has been traditionally thought of as the province of the mother. This of course depends upon how actively involved the father (or for that matter an older sibling) actually is in the care of the baby, but it opens up the possibility of the transition from a two-person to a three- (or more) person world being a very early phenomenon.

Samuels further suggests that it is important for the daughter to experience a profound connection to her father which has an erotic component. Father and daughter are in a sense complete opposites, both in age and gender. The importance for the daughter lies in being loved and appreciated in a non-exploitative way by such a 'different' person. If a girl does not experience this deep and erotic tie with a man with whom she feels quite safe, her personality may fail to be enriched and to grow. If, on the other hand, this relationship actually becomes sexualized, then the girl will come to feel that her sexuality is dangerous and destructive.

In the course of our work with bulimic women, we have repeatedly come across a number of situations in which it was impossible for the daughter to experience her relationship with her father as positive and helpful. Sometimes the relationship between the parents had been so tense and precarious that the father was not able to form a helpful bond with his daughter. Instead he remained a distant figure who was not able to encourage or confirm her as an attractive woman able to take her own place in the world. Alternatively, we have come across a number of instances in which the ties between father and daughter were too strong, too sexualized, and the daughter was in fact exploited by the father or father substitute. Recent research findings from Rhoda Oppenheimer and Robert Palmer[11] suggest that a history of incest or sexual abuse within the family plays a part in the histories of many women who later suffer from bulimia. Of course, knowing the damaging effects of such early experiences, one would expect the victims of sexual abuse to suffer from a range of difficulties later on in life, including bulimia. Further research will no doubt show whether such experiences predispose women towards bulimia in particular.

Family Patterns

While it is always dangerous to make generalizations about families we have nonetheless been struck by the recurrence of certain sorts of patterns which seem to be relevant to the development of the symptom of bulimia.

Whenever we talk about families, we have to keep in

mind that there is really no such thing as an objective account of a family. Any information about a particular family is always mediated through the perceptions of one of its members. In the family patterns we are about to present and discuss, the information is all derived from the family member who went on to develop bulimia. What we are in effect seeing here is not only a series of facts about the family, but how the family has been understood by the member who is narrating the story. Sometimes what we make of our families can be as illuminating as the stories themselves.

Sometimes family members *idealize* their families. They insist that everything at home is or was fine. They talk about people being 'close' and 'caring' and always say with relief that the family has 'no problems'. While not all families have serious difficulties, any situations in which people live together will have their share of difficult and unpleasant experiences and will certainly have to be able to accommodate all the bad feelings which are a part of human nature as well as the good ones. In our experience, women in an anorexic phase will often idealize their families, denying that anything at all difficult ever happened there. We can well understand this need to idealize. The anorexic woman is denying that anything unpleasant or difficult exists in herself. She denies that she has needs or desires, is unable to acknowledge that she can be moved or upset.

The bulimic woman, on the other hand, is able to acknowledge that everything is not perfect. She is often able to talk about things in her family which went wrong and which were sad. What she has difficulty in doing is allowing herself to have any bad feelings about her family and what happened there.

From the number of bulimic women we have worked

with, we are inclined to think that these women's families probably had more than their fair share of difficulties. We have come across very few women who have not experienced at least one major problem in the course of growing up. We have seen a large number of women who have lost a parent, either by divorce or death, a high incidence of mentally ill parents and a number of cases of incest. There is nothing very remarkable in that; many young people have to deal with such difficulties in the course of their development and they certainly don't all suffer from symptoms like bulimia. The difference in these families, and the point which seemed to make them such potentially dangerous places to grow up, is that these were families which didn't expect their children to be upset by what went on. Not only was there no encouragement for these children to talk about their feelings, but usually they were told they shouldn't have any!

The mother of a client of ours died while she was still young. The death was not talked about, feelings were not expressed. Instead, the little girl was sent away to her grandmother for a few days. When she returned home, everything carried on as normal. There was no mention of the fact of her mother's death, no explanation, no mourning.

One of the women who worked with us in a group grew up with a mother whose serious mental illness led to her intolerable neglect. Instead of providing her with an alternative source of care, her father would always warn her against any expression of feeling about her mother, especially anger. He impressed upon her that her mother was ill, and that she had no right to be angry with her. Furthermore, any expression of feeling on her part would be bound to make her mother worse.

Thus the child grew up, understandably full of anxiety and anger about her mother's abandonment of her. If ever she allowed herself to become conscious of these feelings, she would feel guilty, as though she were making her mother worse and therefore being the one to blame in the situation.

Another, even more dramatic example is a young woman, overtly very attractive and making a successful career in one of the helping professions. During her work in the group it transpired that she had had a long-standing incestuous relationship with her father. Although her mother never acknowledged the relationship, she would send the child to sleep in her father's bed as a punishment if she had been 'naughty'. Far from being able to go to her mother for rescue from this sexual abuse, she was given the perfectly clear message that anything which happened to her was her own fault and responsibility and that her own feelings about it were quite inappropriate. We know how important it is that children who have been sexually abused by their parents are allowed and encouraged to talk about what has happened to them and to have their own feelings validated. They also need to be clearly told that what has happened to them is not their own fault. This child had exactly the opposite experience and had to make a precarious compromise into adulthood, keeping inside herself not only all her own feelings associated with the incest, but also the knowledge that it was really her fault.

Sometimes, with the best of intentions, families inhibit the spontaneous expression of feelings and even make their daughters suppress the feelings themselves. One of our clients, a black woman, had been adopted as a baby by a white family and brought up in a part of the north of England where there were no other black people. The family, anxious to avoid any difficulties attaching to having a black child, stressed that there was no difference between black and white, no possible reason for their little daughter to feel anything but one of them. Thus the black child was raised as a white child, in a colour-blind household, where her real difference and individuality could not be acknowledged. The little girl of course perceived herself as really being different, but as she could not talk about it, internalized her feelings of differentness and felt they were something to be ashamed of. Her own real and *different* needs – such as hair and skin care – were ignored or judged as inappropriate. After all, if everyone is really the same, how can anyone have special needs? In this family, we can see that by wanting to protect both their daughter and themselves from the inevitable difficulties of adopting someone from a different cultural and racial background, they effectively forced the child to deal with the problems secretly and alone. This is the way she has continued to deal with difficulties all her life and it is why bulimia was, for her, such an obvious and such an addictive solution.

Another woman in one of the groups had parents who had divorced and remarried another couple, with whom they had previously been friends. This is probably not such an unusual occurrence and need not necessarily be a damaging one. However, it is an event in the lives of children, a complete change and switch in whom to regard as parents, about which each child will have enormously strong and conflicting feelings. In this particular family, the children were expected to behave as though nothing very much had happened. The adults handled it all in a very 'civilized' way and expected the children to do the same. They were told that they had no reason to be upset; that nothing bad or difficult had happened and that their feelings of loss and confusion were inappropriate. This pattern occurs over and over again: a family with its difficulties, where the young woman concerned is not allowed to express or experience the feelings and emotions appropriate to the difficulties. Indeed, what we usually find is that she has been expected to have quite different feelings from the ones which were really hers.

A child is not able to stand back and evaluate what she is being expected to do. Instead, she believes that what her parents say is right and that her own feelings are 'wrong' and bad. Even when a child is treated unfairly and is seriously deprived of care, her dependence on the very people who treat her so badly makes her feel as though she must be the one who is to blame. If the adults don't care for her, she must be unlovable. She is too dependent on the care-takers to contemplate the idea that there might be something wrong with them. Her unconscious explanation to herself is that there is something fundamentally wrong and bad within her. This is exactly the point at which the bulimic woman is stuck. She is unable to evaluate what happens to her. She feels at the mercy of her own feelings and if these don't correspond with what is expected of her, she believes that they are wrong and bad, emanating from a badness deep inside herself.

Boys and Girls

Both boys and girls may be subjected to the kinds of difficulties within their families which we have been describing. Why is it then that boys on the whole seem less likely to produce symptoms, and even when they do, these symptoms rarely centre on food?

Over and over again, we discover that it is not merely what happens to individuals that determines whether or not they have difficulties in later life. Indeed, if it were, we could look at someone's life experiences and predict exactly what difficulties they would have. Clearly we cannot do this. As well as the actual circumstances of a child's life, we also have to consider what the child is able to do with its experience and, in particular, what place that experience has in the child's inner world.

In general, in the case of little girls we find that they are less likely than boys to be able to express their feelings about what has happened to them in an angry way – a problem which confronts professionals working with sexually abused children all the time. Anger can be a very healing emotion for children, as it allows bad feelings to be expressed and dealt with outside the individual. Girls are encouraged not to express angry or difficult feelings, with the result that they are more likely to internalize and keep their feelings inside themselves.

Even when boys do end up with very negative feelings about themselves, there are still, in our society, many more opportunities for boys and men to enhance their self-esteem in the world. We can probably all think of men who compensate for feelings of personal insecurity and difficulties in relationships by becoming very successful in their jobs. Women sometimes do this too, but there are fewer opportunities and the expectation still exists that women will be successful in their personal lives as well. Men do, of course, sometimes produce symptoms of distress, though these are much less often recognized as psychological or psychiatric problems than they are in women. They may well be expressed as physical signs of stress, like ulcers or heart attacks. For women, with their close connection with food and their tendency to regard the body as a source of confirmation and self-esteem, eating disorders are an obvious way of expressing distress and unhappiness. As we have explained in Chapter 2, bulimia is in this sense an over-determined symptom for women. It has its origins both in the particular life experiences of the individual and in the social situation in which women find themselves.

REFERENCES

1. In the section which follows, we are heavily indebted to Harry Guntrip's chapter, 'The Schizoid Personality and the External World', in Guntrip, H., *Schizoid Phenomena, Object Relations and the Self*, The Hogarth Press, London, 1968.
2. Guntrip, *op. cit.*
3. Guntrip, *op. cit.*
4. Fairbairn, W. R. D., 'A Revised Psychopathology of the Psychoses and Psychoneuroses', *Int. J. Psych-Anal*, 22, 1941. Quoted in Guntrip, *op. cit.*
5. Eichenbaum, Luise and Orbach, Susie, *Understanding Women*, Penguin, Harmondsworth, 1983.
6. Flax, Jane, 'The Conflict Between Nurturance and Autonomy in Mother-Daughter Relationships and Within Feminism', in Howell, E., and Bayes, M. (eds), *Women and Mental Health*, Basic Books, New York, 1981.
7. Miller, Alice, *The Drama of the Gifted Child and the Search for the True Self*, Faber, London, 1981.
8. *Ibid.*, p. 110.
9. Winnicott, D. W., *The Child, the Family and the Outside World*, Penguin, Harmondsworth, 1964.
10. Samuels, A. (ed), *The Father: Contemporary Jungian Perspectives*, Free Association Books, London, 1985.

11. Oppenheimer, R., Palmer, R. L., and Stretch, D. (unpublished paper), 'Incest and Anorexia Nervosa', International Symposium on Eating Disorders, Jerusalem, 1986.

CHAPTER 6

Femininity and Creativity: Dealing with the Messy Side of Life

If we are to be able to understand the particularly addictive quality of the symptom of bulimia, the way in which women cling to it in spite of loathing it, we have to understand that in psychological terms it fulfils a positive function. We are not suggesting that this kind of self-damaging behaviour is really a good thing, but rather that in the lives of many women it does fill a gap or provide a bridge in their psychic experience. It gives them a link to their own inner experience which would otherwise be lost.

In this chapter, we shall be looking at some of the ways in which women's socialization can result in their becoming 'out of touch' with an aspect of themselves.

One of the most essential and fundamental components of femininity is a quality which hasn't really got a name. It is related to neatness, to tidyness and cleanness. It has to do with both organization and self-containment. It is such a taken-for-granted aspect of what we have come to regard as woman's 'proper', 'natural' endowment that it is not an attribute we normally need to give a name to. It is a quality which is often defined by its opposite. That opposite is messiness.

From the very earliest age, little girls are taught to dread being messy. As a baby, the little girl may find her face and hands are aggressively wiped at every opportunity. Smearing and playing with food will be firmly discouraged, while her 'successes' in toilet training are warmly applauded. Boy babies too are encouraged to be clean, but not with the same seriousness and fervour as girls. A certain amount of untidiness, even wilful messiness, is tolerated in boys with a degree of amused acceptance. Being messy can even be seen as 'boyish', a positive component in the boy's sexual identity. In this sense, girls and boys inhabit very different worlds. The world of the little girl is one in which keeping clean, tidy and well-organized is likely to be experienced as one of the most stringent demands to be placed upon her.

Being tidy is not portrayed to girls as a quality which has any particular use or purpose. Not being 'messy' is simply assumed to be an essential component of being a little girl. Some of the injunctions against messiness are connected with personal appearance. 'Look at your cardigan! How did it get grubby like that?' The little girl is expected to feel shamed. Others have to do with eating. Eating, at least for small children, seems by its very nature to be a rather messy activity. The series of rules with which we hedge children about at mealtimes seems to be an attempt on the part of adults to bring civilization to bear on this essentially instinctual activity. Although boys and girls alike are subject to the full weight of adult notions of good 'table manners', for a boy to be a messy eater does not carry the same consequence as it does for a girl. 'That's not very ladylike, is it, Samantha?'

There is no equivalent challenge to Sam's sexual

identity which could be levelled at him if he too talked with his mouth full. In the area of food, it seems that any action on the part of little girls which reminds the world that eating is a physical and instinctual activity is likely to be censured. 'Don't bolt your food!' 'Don't eat so *fast*!' 'Don't be greedy!'

The same remarks are frequently made to boys too, but for them they are no more than a gentle scolding. For girls they are an accusation. Mothers actually worry if their daughters have large unrestrained appetites and if they care more about satisfying their hunger than about observing the social niceties of behaviour expected at table.

Most primary school teachers agree that little girls have much better table manners than little boys, and for good reason; they have been taught that manners are so much more important for them. To be a messy eater, to have disorderly appetites which show, contradicts some important rules about femininity.

This civilizing of the girl's instinctual behaviour will later on be transferred to her sexuality. She will come to regard and experience sex as an aesthetic activity which she should be able to do 'nicely' rather than as an expression of her own instincts and desires. Her own unrestrained sexuality she regards as messy.

It is commonly agreed that little girls are easier to toilet train than little boys. This is partly because little girls are socialized into a greater degree of compliance and obedience than little boys. They are encouraged to be responsive to other people's wishes and demands rather than to be adventurous and self-directed, as might be encouraged in their brothers. They are also taught that 'making a mess' is a very, very bad thing for them to do. Little girls know that they are rewarded when they are clean, neat and in control of themselves.

At school, the work which little girls produce tends to be much neater than that of the little boys. They take more *care*, make fewer mistakes and present their work in a tidier way. Again, this is because they are taught that it is very important for them to keep things neat and tidy. Teachers, unconsciously, have higher expectations of the neatness of girls' work. They are less willing to tolerate untidiness in girls' work than they are in boys'. A boy's work is much more likely to be judged on its content, the presentation being generally overlooked. Girls, on the other hand, are absolutely *expected* to present neat work. In all-girl schools, the virtues of tidiness are traditionally extolled. This is not just because it is easier to find things if you keep tidy, but because tidiness is an integral aspect of female socialization. This is what is continually being judged. Boys are not judged in the same terms; indeed, a boy who shows a particular preoccupation with order and neatness may be regarded as unhealthily obsessional, while the same trait would be thought praiseworthy in a girl.

As well as following parental and educational injunctions to avoid being messy, little girls also watch and imitate their mothers. And what do mothers do? They clean and tidy up after people! Whatever else mothers do, and whatever their own natural characteristics and preferences may be, they all spend a good deal of their time and energy imposing order on other people's chaos, and hygiene on other people's dirt.

After the infant has finished playing with her bricks, and before she is old enough to be told to tidy up, she watches her mother putting them away. It is mother

—

who changes nappies, who cleans up the baby, washes away the dirt and disorder. Little girls have toys which replicate the real domestic appliances used by their mothers: toy irons, with which, like mother, they smooth out the wrinkles and make clothes nice and neat to wear; they use toy brushes and dustpans, even toy hoovers.

Some mothers, especially those who do all their work within the home, become very skilled at clearing up after other people. As one woman told us, 'My father thinks he's very tidy. In fact it's just that whatever he throws down, my mother picks up before it hits the floor and he thinks he's done it all himself!' Women who share more economic equality with their male partners often insist on a more equal division of domestic labour, so that all the family members take on a share of the clearing-up work. However, it is nearly always mother who feels responsible for seeing that clearing up gets done. If guests come unexpectedly and two days' washing-up is in the sink, the rubbish needs emptying and there isn't a chair clear of things to sit on, it will probably be mother who feels guilty and responsible, as though she has somehow failed in her duties. In fact, of course, she has not eaten all the food to make the washing-up; not all the rubbish is hers and she is not the only able-bodied person in the house. Yet she is still likely to feel that the visitors will pass judgement on her. And she will probably be right.

Many women, especially those who do most of their work within the home, experience life as a continual struggle against themselves. All the time they are striving to be the perfect immaculate home-maker. But always, other women's kitchens look tidier, cleaner, more organized than their own. Other women's children don't look so grubby! Some women, on the other hand, feel that in housework, through the task of taking care of and ordering a home and a family, they have finally overcome their messy natures. As young girls competing in the world of 'dating', 'being fancied' and finally finding a partner, she may have felt big, clumsy, inept and altogether a mess. She may feel that as a home-maker and housekeeper, she has finally found her own feminine ability and competence. Sometimes when women find that their sense of self-esteem is threatened, when they feel unsure of their worth and value as women, they retreat more and more into the pursuit of perfection within their homes. In a quite obsessive way, the task of keeping an orderly environment becomes all-important. We need to understand this as both an attempt to deal with internal feelings of disorder, and also a retreat into what as women we have been taught to believe is the 'right' way to be.

What then are the psychological effects of this early socialization? How do we as adult women reflect what we have been taught about the necessity to avoid being messy?

The short answer is that we learn to repress, to hold down or *hide* the parts of our personalities which will be thought to be messy. We do this in terms of repressing our own natural untidiness, but at another level we learn to hide our distress, our confusion and uncertainty; anything in fact which will disturb the orderly exterior which we feel we must present to the world. Anything which has to do with the expression of spontaneous feeling, anything which threatens to spill over, anything which signifies loss of control – all these things we learn to suppress and deny within ourselves.[1]

If we think back to the hungry baby described in the

previous chapter and remember how her ordinary neediness tended to be regarded as inappropriate and over-demanding, we can see how this very neediness becomes associated with loss of control, with a lack of self-containment. Needs, when they can be experienced and given voice to at all, must only be met in a measured and partial way, never allowing them full expression or resolution. The bulimic women we work with tell us over and over again that they dare not acknowledge how needy they feel, for if they did, they might become like helpless babies, insatiable and unconsolable.

The very fact that this kind of emotional self-containment is so valued as a feminine attribute makes it very difficult for women in contemporary society to get their emotional needs acknowledged and met. This is one of the central dilemmas facing the post-modern woman, the woman who has freed herself to an extent from the constrictions which bound her mother and grand-mother. Very often women ask us, 'What is the point of getting in touch with my real needs? No one is going to meet them for me!' All too often, they are right!

Bulimia is one of the most effective symptoms women have devised for both *expressing* and at the same time *containing and hiding* their neediness, messiness and their inability to hold everything together, and keep everything in. It is in itself a very messy symptom. The uncontrolled, uncontained, 'crazy' part of the woman is, through the bulimic ritual, acknowledged and confirmed. The way she eats is messy, disgusting, out of control. Then she makes herself sick, making another mess. But of course, the mess itself is limited, contained, and cleaned up again before anyone can find out! In the same way, the woman experiences herself as crazy, perverted, disgusting and 'sick' – but only for a limited time, and in secret. What she is effectively doing is keeping alive the part of herself which has not succumbed to the pressures to tidy up her inner world. Interestingly enough, this hidden and tormented part of the woman often turns out to be her creative self.

Chaos and Creativity

When we as women, at an early age, learn to repress and subdue our innate messiness, we are also, unwittingly, repressing our own creativity. To make this statement a little clearer, let us first try to say something about what 'creativity' actually is, and how it is developed within the individual. All of us, as human beings, have to contend with our inner world, consisting of all our own individual and personal feelings and perceptions, both conscious and unconscious. This personal world, constructed out of some of our earliest and most primitive experiences, remembered and unremembered, contributes a good deal to making us the distinctive individuals we turn out to be. In addition, we all have, of course, to live within the social world, the 'real' world, as it is sometimes called, of *shared* experience. In truth, our inner worlds are no less real, though they may be more difficult to describe or communicate about. To some extent, these two worlds are always in a state of conflict or tension. The inner world has to take account only of the needs, longings and wishes of the individual; only the experience of the person herself is real. The social world, on the other hand, the world of shared experience, may pay very little attention to the experience of that particular individual. It is a world which is often experienced as demanding, impinging, rather than enabling or understanding. As adult people, we all have to find ways of accommodating to the realities and demands of the external world. In this we really have no choice. But we also have the task of keeping in touch with and maintaining a respect for our own inner worlds, which may sometimes pull us in quite different directions.

Creativity could be described as the personal ability to find some space between these worlds; to allow the inner reality to take over for a while and impose itself upon what is outside us. This is not to lose all awareness of the external reality, but simply the capacity to become preoccupied with inner things in a way which allows them to be expressed and made real and concrete in the world outside. This space between the inner world of the individual and the social, external world, the psychoanalyst Winnicott calls 'potential space'.[2] We might say for example that the artist has found the capacity to put on to canvas visual images which arise in her inner world in such a way that they are available and understandable in some way to people outside herself. In the process of her creativity she inhabits her own potential space, outside of her inner world, yet not quite a part of the world outside herself. As Winnicott understands it, we first discover and explore our potential space through play.

Playing, for Winnicott, is the sign that the child, however stressed she may be in other ways, is still able to keep alive her inner world and the reality outside her, and to find a way of expressing herself in the territory in between the two. Playing, he believes, is the infantile expression of that capacity which we will later be able to use to participate in the culture and civilization in which we find ourselves. In other words, playing is the first expression of our creativity.

Perhaps the most disastrous consequence of the socialization of small girls is the crucial importance of neatness and tidiness in that it inhibits their ability to play.

Play, by its very nature, is often messy. This is recognized by child psychologists, and indeed by nursery nurses and nursery school teachers. They will go to great lengths to provide for children the essentially messy substances of sand, water, clay and paint. The sad fact is that while we offer little girls messy things to play with, we also offer them toys which have to do with clearing up. There is sand on the one hand, and the toy vacuum cleaner on the other. It is not the toys themselves which have the effect of eradicating the potential creativity of little girls. Rather, they serve as the symbols for what is really going on. It is no coincidence that the 'feminine' or 'womanly' arts or expressions of creativity have confined themselves traditionally to needlework, to the copying of flowers or plants, or the acquisition of calligraphic skills. Neither should it surprise us that there are comparatively few women artists. The sampler, perhaps the high point of female creativity in the Victorian era, is a clear expression of the ways in which it was felt female creativity should be expressed. Female creativity is understood as neat, clean, tidy, precisely controlled and with unequivocal boundaries. This is not a way in which any human being could possibly express her inner reality. And yet if we compare this to the social reality with which women are confronted, we can see that it corresponds well. What women are expected to do, and indeed we do do, is not only to *behave* in ways which will be all about not making a mess – being neat, taking care, clearing up – but we also impose these strictures upon our own inner reality.

By limiting our own possibilities of making a mess, we restrict our own likelihoods of creating a masterpiece.

Bulimia and Creativity

What are we suggesting? That bulimia is really creative? No, not exactly that, but that bulimia does occupy the *same space* in women's lives as her potential creativity. In that space between the world of her inner reality and the constraints of the outside world, instead of creativity we find a self-destructive symptom. But the important point is that in the bulimic woman this space *does exist*. She is not so overwhelmed by the demands of the 'real world' that she has completely lost touch with the spontaneous, feeling and rebellious parts of herself. Instead of being able to integrate and feel positive about this part of her which she feels most real, she shuts it away and makes it into something shameful and secretive.

One clear implication of what we are saying is that part of the process of giving up her bulimic symptoms and way of life may involve the woman in the rediscovery of her own essential creativity and the beginnings of a new way of expressing it. For some women, this means giving up the struggle to achieve perfection through keeping everything neat and tidy and instead finding the space to play – whatever that might mean for the individual woman concerned. While some women feel frustrated with their lives as housewives, the cleaners-up and organizers of others, such a role can also convey a sense of safety, both from the conflicts of the outside world and her own inner conflicts. On a positive note, we have observed over the years that many of the bulimic women who come seeking help are already struggling with their own creativity. We have worked with women who have outstanding talents, particularly in the fields of art and literature, and the development of these potentials can be a vital part of the healing process.

REFERENCES

1. Graham, Hilary, 'Coping, or How Mothers are Seen and Not Heard', in Friedman, S. and Sarah, E. (eds), *On the Problem of Men*, The Women's Press, London, 1982.
2. Winnicott, D. W., *Playing and Reality*, Tavistock, London, 1971.

CHAPTER 7

The Good and the Bad

The dichotomy of good and bad within us and in the world around us has been predominant from the dawn of human existence. It is a recurring theme in the Bible, in both Western and Eastern philosophy, in mythology, literature and all religions. Both God and the Devil, good and evil, are external entities which also affect and reflect the internal worlds of us all. The purpose behind all this speculation is always clearly stated: to strive for the good and to avoid the bad. We are extolled to do all we can to be good and in return we are promised a reward either immediately, or perhaps delayed a little — such as going to heaven or achieving Nirvana. If we should choose the bad path, we are warned of inevitable punishment. The bad, although given very negative associations, has a seductive and tempting quality to it. It may be one's purpose in life to overcome this temptation, but it is not put forward as an easy task and it is expected to be a struggle. If the good wins out, the reward awaits.

There is a very clear assumption here that good is good, that bad is bad and that there is no confusion or overlap between the two. They are seen as two entities, very clearly separate from each other. In our spiritual as well as our temporal lives, it is supposed to be very easy to tell the difference between good and bad. Volumes of rules are written down and even more are unwritten; injunctions spoken and unspoken are somehow passed down through the generations about what it is good to be and do and think and feel, and what is bad.

Stereotypes of goodness, rules, conventions and norms obviously affect us all, but in a patriarchal culture it seems that women are more bound by being 'good' – pure and unselfish – than men are. It seems to be women's role as mothers which colours and determines the shoulds and oughts in their lives. There are other very specific ways in which women are damaged and oppressed by the rules and stereotypes of femininity which will be discussed elsewhere. Here we are concentrating on the injunctions on women which are to do with good and bad.

Patriarchal culture contains a completely unreal image of the perfectly good woman. She is both a good mother and also a virgin. She is pure and giving, loving and caring. Her opposite is the whore, the dirty, bad woman, rejected by society. Both of these extremes have their own assumptions and characteristics attaching to them. The good woman is beautiful, quiet, well-behaved, caring, giving, unassertive, unassuming and obedient. She is also clean and thin, always looking and smelling good. She has an ethereal, spiritual quality to her which puts her above the mere concerns of the body. The bad woman, on the other hand, is animal-like; she has desires which she fulfils. She is dirty, aggressive, loud and sexual.

These two stereotypes are conveyed to us through

films, literature and, for many of us until recently, through our families and the models of women around us. The reward, so we are led to believe, for being a good woman is marriage and a family, while isolation, instability and loneliness are the lot of the bad woman, particularly in her later years when even her good looks desert her.

Over and over again, the bulimic women we work with express their real fear of this image of the 'bad' woman, and the absolute conviction that underneath the 'good' exterior, the bad woman lives inside them. Our reality as human beings is that we have both good and bad feelings and thoughts. Much as we might prefer not to, we have to accept the reality of both these forces inside ourselves and in the external world.

We all want to have good, positive, pleasurable feelings about ourselves and about other people. In our imaginations, we long for a situation where only good feelings exist; in reality we have to reconcile and accept the existence of both good and bad.

When we talk about 'bad' feelings, what we usually mean are feelings which we have been taught to reject. It is not that feelings such as anger, envy, hostility and sexual desire are actually 'bad' in themselves. In a sense, feelings aren't really capable of being good or bad; only actions can be subject to moral judgement. And yet so terrified can we become of the possible outcome of our feelings, so afraid that we will lose control of ourselves, that we try to cut these possibilities off at their source and make ourselves and our children afraid and ashamed of our feelings. One way of dealing with our bad feelings is to split them off from the good ones and to put them in a well-defined corner of our lives. This corner we then label bad and we do not have to deal with bad feelings getting in the way of, or messing up, or affecting the rest of life.

A woman who grew up with these two conflicting stereotypes of the good and bad woman will have discovered very early on that her feelings towards others include not just care, love and altruism, but also anger, hate and contempt. How can she deal with her desires, with her emerging sexuality? With her body, which becomes strangely out of her control, producing curves and hair and unwanted substances – blood and mucus? She was taught that little girls are made of sugar and spice; she never expected to have to contend with feelings like this and, of course, she believes that other girls don't have them. Separating good from bad as a solution to these dilemmas is not a new idea. It is a way of pursuing a form of pure goodness, unaffected by badness and purified by the separation.

Jekyll and Hyde

In the original story of Dr Jekyll and Mr Hyde, we find that the Doctor's initial motivation to split off the part of himself which later became the autonomous Mr Hyde was precisely in order to keep the bad part of himself separate from the good.

Dr Jekyll was a well-known and successful physician, a studious and popular man who was renowned for his good works. Such a perfectionist was Dr Jekyll that he began to regard the aspects of himself which were committed to less serious pursuits as in some way evil and not able to be integrated into the one identity. As he tells his story, 'Hence it came about that I concealed my pleasures and that when I reached years of reflection and began to look around me and take stock of my progress and position in the world, I stood committed to a profound duplicity of life.'[1] It was not that Dr Jekyll's 'pleasures' were in truth particularly sinful or unusual, 'but from the high views that I had set before me, I regarded and hid them with an almost morbid sense of shame'. Trying to make sense of these two very different aspects of his nature, Dr Jekyll wrote, 'With every day ... I drew steadily nearer to the truth ... that man is not truly one, but truly two.' So for the 'good' doctor, the solution to his personal moral dilemma seems to be found in the acknowledgement of the dualistic nature of humankind, and the importance of keeping the dual aspects separate. 'I began to dwell on the thought of the separation of these elements. If each could be housed in separate identities, life would be relieved of all that was unbearable.'[2]

He records the way in which, for a time, this separation of the good and the bad worked for him, but it was not to last. For a long while the struggle went on between those two selves, till the day came when Jekyll could no longer control his other self and Mr Hyde would reappear without Jekyll needing to take the drug he had created for the purpose. 'I began to be tortured with throes and longings ... My devil had been long caged; he came out roaring.'

The bulimic woman, like the unfortunate Dr Jekyll, is a perfectionist. She wants her spiritual nature to be free of any human flaws. Like him, she attempts to split off the bad from the good in her life. This, for the modern woman, is often symbolized by the ability to eat only 'good' foods. Thus, bulimia initially looks like the perfect solution; she really can have her cake and eat it. She can have her fill – vast amounts of food; she can succumb to her overwhelming needs, shut them up with a binge and yet not have to carry the consequence with the fat showing on her body. She can present the good Dr Jekyll, and the bad Mr Hyde indeed remains hidden. However, as in the original story, it does not take long for the hidden side to begin to take control. Like Mr Hyde who began to emerge uncalled for, the solution she has found seems to prove less and less effective. The more these human needs and feelings are pushed aside, the more they try to burst out and the more violent is their struggle to do so. And the more threatening and overwhelming they seem to the woman herself.

Many bulimic women say, 'I have no problems apart from this horrible eating and vomiting, which has been going on for the past three (or four or six or twenty) years.' The bulimia is a separate, hidden part, which encapsulates 'the problems' in her life; like a bubble, where all the unacceptable, problematic, hated and feared aspects of herself are lodged. Her statement, 'If only I were not bulimic everything would be all right,' is confirmed by this situation. All her 'badness' is pushed away and centred on her bulimia; all her uneasy and painful feelings are blamed on the symptom. All her bad, needy, angry, dependent aspects become attached to the bulimia, so that they are not directly experienced. This encapsulated bubble allows her to lead quite a 'normal' life where she can present herself as 'good'.

The woman's behaviour symbolizes the way in which she deals with the 'bad' aspects of herself. The toilet or the bathroom is the one room in which she will allow her 'mess' to spill over. Behind the locked door of that room, she allows herself to vomit, to get dirty, to smell bad, to do everything that is unacceptable, hateful and disgusting to her. The good side of her is the person who does not make demands, who does not get angry or aggressive. She has no bodily needs or desires, and eats only healthy food in small quantities. The 'bad' side is overwhelming – too much for people, and hateful and disgusting. The 'bad' woman is the one who is obsessed with eating and vomiting; she has needs and smells and is dirty.

The Contribution of Melanie Klein[3]

Melanie Klein was a psychoanalyst who pioneered the use of play therapy with children. Her work focuses particularly on the inner life of the individual during the earliest stages of life. We offer here a short account of her ideas and how we think they might be helpful in understanding bulimia. Some people find these ideas helpful and illuminating, while others consider them rather strange and speculative. We have included this account because it seems to us that Klein has some important things to say about good and bad and our ways of dealing with them. We fully appreciate, however, that this might not be everyone's 'cup of tea'! We invite the reader therefore to take a look at this material for its stimulating qualities without necessarily feeling that all of the ideas have to be immediately accepted.

Klein is interested in the primitive phantasies* of the very small baby. She sees the baby as dominated by overpowering feelings of both love and hate towards

---

* Following the usual convention the 'ph' spelling is used to indicate that the process is unconscious.

the mother. At this very early stage of life, all the baby's feelings are focused on the feeding process, which is the primary source of both satisfaction and frustration. It is thus the breast, which is the part of the mother experienced by the baby, which is the recipient of all the loving and hating feelings of the baby.

When the feeding goes well and the baby is fed at the right time, just when she is hungry, if the milk flows just as she wants it to, not too fast and not too slow, then the baby can direct her loving feelings towards the breast. If, on the other hand, she is kept waiting for a feed and becomes fretful and upset, if she swallows too fast and chokes on the milk, if the breast seems dry and she has to suck too hard, then all her hateful, angry and destructive feelings are turned towards the breast. Indeed, according to Klein, even if the baby has only good experiences of feeding, she will still, at times, feel deprived and angry. In her phantasy, the baby attacks the breast, trying to suck it dry, bite it up and scoop out all its good contents. The difficulty the baby has with her aggressive phantasies, her bad feelings, is that she is both afraid that she will destroy the breast, her source of satisfaction and nurturance, and also afraid that the breast will retaliate and destroy her. In order to protect herself from the possible consequences of these bad feelings, the baby uses the defence we know as *projection*. In other words, she disowns the feelings herself and instead puts them on to the breast itself. She can then believe that it is not she who wishes to destroy the breast, but the bad breast which wants to destroy her. She then has a phantasy of a bad, destructive force, which is external to herself. She is not troubled by all these bad feelings within her. In the same way, by keeping the breast separated into two aspects, good and bad, the baby can retain the good breast, the aspect of the mother which she experiences as loving and satisfying, without it having to come into contact with or be in any way spoiled by the bad breast. This defence is called *splitting*.

As well as projecting her bad feelings on to the phantasy of the breast, the baby also introjects what she perceives or experiences of the external object. Thus she will take in as part of herself, both the good object – the loving and satisfying breast – and the bad object – the persecuting and vengeful breast. The defence of splitting also operates in an internal way, so that the ego itself is split into a good part which is kept entirely separate from the bad part.

Klein describes this as part of the normal process of infant development. The next stage in development, and indeed the great challenge in development, is for the baby to become able to take in the whole person with both good and bad aspects and thus to accept that good and bad can exist together, alongside each other, without the good being destroyed by the bad. If conditions are favourable for the baby, she will move on to this next position and in the process will be able to experience remorse for her destructive phantasies towards the breast as well as the will to repair and restore the mother who can be loved in spite of her faults. At this stage she is also able to experience the 'good' and 'bad' in herself and to have a sense of herself as, while not perfect, not totally evil either.

Even if development continues in this way, all of us still retain the defences which are used by the tiny baby. We all, sometimes, project our own feelings on to other people and become overwhelmed by a sense of our own badness.

In serious forms of mental illness such as schizophrenia, these defences again assume a very dominant position and the psychotic individual is unable to distinguish his own projections from the actual behaviour of other people, just like the tiny baby with the breast. The woman who develops a symptom like bulimia, while in some respects having matured beyond these very early defences, may still feel insecure in her ability to integrate goodness and badness. Sometimes she can have a sense of herself and other people as a complex mixture of love and hate, while at other moments she has a sense of being quite overwhelmed by her own badness.

In many ways, bulimia represents and acts out these very primitive defences. In order to retain any sense of her own goodness, the woman with this kind of symptom needs to keep it separate and apart from everything which she feels to be bad. Just like Dr Jekyll, she feels that her badness, her imperfection, always threatens to attack and annihilate anything good within her. She projects on to the symptom of bulimia everything which is bad within herself, in her life or which originates within other people in just the same way as the infant projects everything bad on to the 'bad' breast. We need to understand both the small baby's creation of the bad breast and the adult woman's creation of a symptom like bulimia as attempts to keep all the bad things together in one place, under control. This enables the good breast, the idealized mother, to be preserved and the internalized goodness, the sense of being good, to be kept away from all the badness inside.

We can understand the bulimic woman's frantic devouring of huge amounts of food as an attempt on her part to take in the good and nourishing breast just as she had partially succeeded in introjecting it in infancy. But having done that, the internalized bad object, the bad breast which she has introjected and which she now experiences as within herself, as soon as it comes in contact with the food, turns it bad too. What she is dealing with is her own feeling of destructiveness, her sense of having destroyed, torn and bitten up the breast, which she now experiences as evil and poisonous inside her, turning bad everything which she takes in. The only hope now is to get rid of the bad food, to project it out, just as the original bad feelings were projected on to the mother.

We might now want to ask why it is that some individuals seem to be able to progress through this stage where good and bad need to be split and reach a point where they are able to see both themselves and other people in an integrated way so that good and bad can coexist. There is no simple answer to such a question, and there is certainly no universal agreement as to what makes for healthy as opposed to unhealthy psychological development. It does seem, though, that we should be looking beyond the internal processes of the infant to the external environment in which the baby finds herself. The psychoanalyst D. W. Winnicott[4] suggests that it is a continuing, unchanging holding of the baby throughout all her many changes of mood and regardless of whatever bad feelings she projects on to the mother which will allow her eventually to see the mother as a whole person. This 'holding' is at the centre of the relationship between mother and infant and implies both a physical care, and also the ability on the part of the mother to 'stay with' the baby in an emotional sense, to contain and make safe all the baby's feelings. So long as the mother is able to provide constant care in the face of the baby's changing mood states, then it becomes possible for the infant to take back some of the projected feelings, to acknowledge that she, not the mother, is sometimes full of anger and rage and that the mother, although not perfect, can be experienced as one being, distinct from the baby.

But what happens if the mother or care-taker is not able to provide this constant and unchanging support? Alice Miller[5] suggests that very many children experience parents who are not at all able to do this. The problem, she believes, lies in the projective processes which flow not from child to mother, but rather the other way round, from parent on to child. Parents themselves often have aspects of their own personalities which they feel are 'bad'. It may be their own anger or envy or sense of failure, for example, which is so painful and distressing to them that they are not able to feel these things. The painful feeling is then split off and can be projected by the parent on to the baby.

Bulimia can be both a means of stifling these bad and disturbing emotions, and also a way of giving them some expression. The symptom itself has a highly dramatic quality: the consuming of vast quantities of food, the 'risk' involved in having to manipulate things to be alone, or else to have to vomit secretly while other people are around; the secrecy, deceit, fear and excitement, the almost sexual quality of the arousal of the body produced by sensations of overeating and vomiting. This is a way of regaining the capacity to feel the intense feelings which she is forced to split off and subdue. She has a sense of emptiness which comes from having lost touch with her true self and true feelings. The bulimia is an expression of that inner life which has had to survive secretly, under the surface, beneath her parents' gaze, throughout her childhood. To express these feelings earlier was to risk losing her parents' affection and love. The repression of these feelings causes her feelings of emptiness and depression – 'If only I wasn't bulimic, my life would be quite happy' – but it also represents a kind of vitality which is encapsulated in an obsessional symptom and which, from there, sends out a cry for help. Since the path to safe verbal communication based on a feeling of trust was blocked for her, the only way she was able to communicate with the world was by means of unconscious enactment – by becoming bulimic.

REFERENCES

1. Stevenson, R. L., *Dr Jekyll and Mr Hyde*, Collins, London, 1953.
2. *Ibid.*
3. See the bibliography for some of Melanie Klein's work on which this account is based.
4. See, for example, Winnicott, D. W., 'The Theory of the Parent-Infant Relationship', in *The Maturational Processes and the Facilitating Environment*, The Hogarth Press, London, 1965.
5. Miller, Alice, *For Your Own Good*, Faber, London, 1983.

CHAPTER 8

A Therapeutic Perspective

In the first part of the book we have looked at what
bulimia is, how the symptom might be understood and
the role it occupies in women's lives. We now turn to
look at what can be done for sufferers and how we can
use our understanding to develop a therapeutic
approach. This chapter explores the issues which will
be important to the bulimic woman at the point at
which she seeks help. In the two following chapters, we
outline the particular therapeutic responses which have
been developed at the Women's Therapy Centre: individual, one-to-one therapy, therapy groups and self-
help groups.

The aim of this section is to provide an account of
therapy which will be of use to therapists, counsellors
and other professionals who may have the opportunity
to work with bulimic women. In addition, and equally
important, we also want to provide a coherent account
of therapy for women who might be thinking of seeking
help with their problem.

One of the things we have learnt is that there is no
one way of offering help to bulimic women. What suits
one woman might not suit another and, anyway, not

everyone has access to all forms of treatment. We hope that by describing a range of treatments we might both help therapists to make more useful assessments and women who are seeking help to make some more informed choices. Of course, we also hope that doctors, counsellors and other professionals who do not now work with bulimic women may be encouraged to do so! One of the greatest difficulties facing women wanting help at present is the sheer lack of resources available.

It is important to say at the outset that, while we share our experience of working with bulimic women and focus on the particular difficulties of involvement both individually and in groups, we make no pretence of offering a comprehensive guide on how to be a therapist. We assume that therapists, counsellors and other professionals will, like us, have their own training and experience which they bring to the particular problem of bulimia.

We are aware that for many women, 'therapy' will be an unfamiliar concept which may seem rather mysterious and off-putting. Part of our purpose, by describing the process of our own work, is to demystify it and make it more accessible.

Bulimia: Personal Problem or Social Problem?

Before we begin to describe and discuss the therapeutic approaches we have found most helpful, we must begin by asking in what sense is it appropriate to treat the bulimic woman as though she is the one with all the problems?

Therapy is, of course, a way of working to alleviate the distress of the individual. As such it concentrates on her experiences, her life, her past, her family and, in psychodynamic therapy, her relationship with the therapist. It may be easy, in taking this very personal and individual focus, to lose sight of the essentially social origins of the problems she faces. While it is simple enough to take account of the social aspects of a problem when writing or thinking about how it occurs, how we should understand it, such a perspective can more easily get lost when it comes to our actual practice. Thus, while we work with women on their own personal distress, looking with them at their childhoods, families, relationships, we are constantly having to grapple with questions such as, How come so many women torment themselves with thoughts, conflicts, feelings about their eating and body size? How are we to understand the particular strand of self-destructiveness which seems to permeate the lives of so many women? Any account of women's eating disorders which does not take these questions into account and try to provide some understanding of them cannot be more than a very incomplete and misleading account.

The fact that therapy is about personal change does not mean, as far as we are concerned, that personal change is all that is needed. It is a sad reflection on contemporary culture that so many women need therapy in order to free them from socially induced difficulties and allow them to lead less troubled lives. There are many deeply held and damaging attitudes and prejudices towards women which will need to change before we can see bulimia as merely a personal problem. In what follows, we are looking at how to work with individual women to bring about change in their lives. This is not necessarily because we think that this is where change should ideally be focused. But it is a fact, and one that we confront constantly, that at the end of the day, it is the woman herself as an individual who carries the pain, and it is with that pain that we must work.

Breaking the Circle

Bulimia is a dark secret. It is a self-contained pattern of behaviour which feeds on itself. An attempt by someone from the outside to break into this pattern, to remove one part of the circle without attending to the rest, to take away the secret without replacing it with something as meaningful will be at best pointless, at worst a disaster. We need to understand bulimia as a containing symptom. It is the 'rubbish bin' which contains and holds for the woman all the unpleasant, dirty, rejected and unacceptable parts of herself. What happens when you take away the rubbish bin, leaving the woman with all her feelings but nothing to contain them?

As we understand it, bulimia is often a symptom which prevents a woman from having a breakdown. Symbolically, locking herself in the bathroom, she breaks down every day. It is vitally important that in our approach to bulimic women we do not just relate to the symptom but also to the role the symptom plays in her life.

Hospital Treatment

We have worked with women who have been admitted to hospital units for their bulimia. Sometimes this has been to ordinary psychiatric units, which may have little specialized knowledge of the problem, sometimes to units specializing in eating disorders. The problem with some of the specialist units we have encountered is that they tend to focus almost exclusively on the eating behaviour. She will be put on a 'regime' designed to 'regulate' her eating. She may be kept in bed, given three large meals a day and attempts will be made to see that she doesn't vomit or have access to laxatives. She will be made to use a commode and the sink in her room will be blocked up. We have heard of many ingenious attempts by women to circumvent these restrictions, such as laxatives hidden in the pepper pot and cleaners bribed to provide extra food for 'binges'. Such a state of affairs seems a waste of time and money. Even if the woman temporarily succeeds in regulating her eating, she will leave hospital with no more understanding of the real nature and origins of her problem or how to cope with it than she had before; and highly vulnerable to developing another, equally destructive symptom.

Some hospital units have a far better understanding of bulimia and provide individual therapy, group work and counselling. This is a great improvement on the rigid regime described above and some of the more enlightened and experienced units provide very high standards of in-patient and out-patient care. They differ from our own approach, however, in that they do not usually take account of the questions we posed earlier on in this chapter. Why women? What is it about being a woman which is so disturbing in our society that women perpetually destroy themselves? Why do women express their most profound pain and fear through their bodies and their eating? It seems to us that an approach to bulimia which does not take these questions into account is a partial one.

It is the theoretical perspective presented throughout the first part of this book which informs our practice as therapists with bulimic women. We can summarize that perspective as follows:

> women are terrified of and despise their
> dependence and other needy parts of themselves;
> women find it hard to care for themselves
> directly, but often do so vicariously by meeting
> the needs of others;
> for women, food is often the currency of their
> caring for others;
> a woman does not learn to love her body, her
> femininity, her sexuality;
> women use their bodies to express distress;
> the complex and unsatisfactory nature of the
> mother/daughter relationship often leaves
> women both terrified of and longing for intimacy
> and care;
> the gender of the therapist is an important
> dynamic in the therapy relationship.

Just as bulimia expresses the ambivalent and conflictual attitude the woman has to herself and her own emotional nurturance, we have come to realize that, symbolically, therapy is a kind of feeding, another sort of nurturance. We understand that the woman may therefore have similar difficulties with therapy as she has with food, and that therapy, whether group or individual, is a helpful arena in which the metaphor of her bulimia can be decoded, understood and integrated in a new way.

What Bulimic Women Bring to Therapy

In the first part of the book, we outlined the issues involved in bulimia. Now we explore the ways in which these issues appear in therapy.

Ambivalence

One of the most important aspects of herself which the bulimic woman brings is her ambivalence, her 'yes, but ... no thank you' attitude. She both wants and yet rejects people, relationships, therapy, good things, herself. This means that she will seek help, both wanting it and not wanting it. Everyone, of course, has doubts and fears when they decide to begin to explore aspects of themselves which they have always hidden and tried to deny. The symptom of bulimia, however, represents a much more deep-seated tendency to simultaneously hold opposing wants and needs. Her ambivalence manifests itself in her taking and throwing away, taking in and throwing out. She may express great distress and despair when she phones the Centre; she is offered an interview and does not turn up. A woman may express her deep need for the group in her interview and then miss most of the sessions of the group itself.

This ambivalent attitude can cause great difficulties. It can, if not acknowledged and talked about, result in the woman rejecting help altogether. We have found, however, that as long as the therapist is able to accept and talk about the way the woman is feeling, it is usually possible for the woman to continue.

Control

Control is an issue for many women. Most women, under our present social arrangements, feel that they do not have a great deal of control over their lives. Women's time tends to be structured around other people's lives – the family's in particular. Bulimic women have only a very precarious sense of being in control of their lives, experiencing themselves as often dependent on the will and wish of others. In addition, bulimia is an expression of feelings of an internal world, a psychological world, which is out of control too. Her feelings, needs, yearnings, rages, all threaten to go out of control at any moment.

Bulimia is a graphic expression of this dynamic. During a 'binge', the woman will often experience herself as two people, the actor and her own onlooker, helpless to prevent what is happening, entirely unable to control herself. At the same time, however, we can understand the self-induced vomiting which follows such a 'binge' as a most dramatic attempt to control the effects of the food. By vomiting out the food, she controls what she experiences as her 'badness'. The more her life feels out of control, the more likely will she be to use the symptom to act out her sense of being out of control and her illusion of regaining it through her vomiting.

In terms of therapy, the bulimic woman will have difficulties with her conflicts about control. Her need to be in control will make it difficult for her when she cannot control the therapist or the other members of the group. She may come late to sessions so that she can feel as though she has some say in when the session starts; she may take her holiday a week after the therapist's break has finished, which gives her the feeling that she is in control of one aspect of the therapy. On the other hand, the powerful and frightening feelings which therapy arouses will make her feel as though she is losing internal control. All this must be discussed and understood within the therapy, either individual or group, so that the woman is enabled, perhaps for the first time, to look at and experience her feelings about control without having to act them out.

Issues Around Boundaries[1]

If we define 'boundary' as the line that separates the 'me' from the 'not me', our own sense of self and of our own boundaries will determine the extent to which we welcome or block certain people, events and experiences in our life. By looking at, and understanding, the way a bulimic woman uses food – by taking it all in in a non-selective and unnourishing way – we can understand that her sense of self and her own boundary is not very clear and strong.

The bulimic woman's boundary is her façade, the image she presents to the world. As she is so concerned with being liked and being thought well of, this boundary remains permeable, allowing in anyone, anything which makes demands on her. At the same time, she has to continue to cover up and conceal the secret 'bad' part of herself; nothing must come too near to that. So at some point, everything which comes in – friendship, care, concern, therapy – must be thrown out, rejected, pushed away.

It is this conflict over her boundaries that the bulimic woman brings to therapy. She brings her two sides, the overt 'good' and the hidden 'bad', with the need to reject everything that comes too close to her hidden 'real' self. As a consequence, any kind of intimacy, with anyone, including the therapist, is absolutely terrifying. It is impossible for a woman to have a helpful relationship with a therapist or group until some of this can be acknowledged. A great deal of time can be wasted by relating exclusively to the 'good' façade which the woman presents, while ignoring what she is concealing. When this happens, she feels forced to reject whatever can be taken in from the therapy immediately afterwards, and in secret – in just the same way as she rejects her food.

Her difficulty with boundaries means that she will often feel furious and frustrated with the boundaries of the therapist or the group. It will sometimes seem unbearable to her that the therapist is not constantly available to her or that the group is a time-limited one. It is obviously very important in these circumstances that the therapist feels confident about her own boundaries and her ability to assert them. She will not only provide an important model for her client, but also, by offering something contained, which is not a 'binge', the client has a valuable experience of something which is limited and yet good.

Sexuality[2]

The bulimic woman also brings to therapy her own painfully confused and conflicting feelings about her sexuality, her femininity and her own body.

It is certainly true that the movement for women's liberation has brought with it a change in attitude towards women's sexuality. Women's sexual activity is no longer regarded as something to be hidden, crushed and confined solely to the institution of marriage. On the contrary: before the current fears about AIDS there was almost an expectation that young women would have a variety of sexual partners. Yet women's bodies are still used and portrayed as sexual objects, still the focus of a cultural obsession with appearance and with thinness.

These contradictory attitudes to women's sexuality tend to mean that although it is no longer denied and denigrated, it is still strictly bound by convention and women's bodies are judged as stringently as they have ever been. Bulimic women in particular seem to have internalized these contradictions. While on the surface many of them appear as sexually 'liberated' women, women who can manage their own sexuality, underneath that is all the uncertainty, the feelings of being judged and many of the 'old-fashioned' feelings of shame and self-disgust. It may take several generations before the external changes in women's lives are internalized and fully integrated into women's internal worlds.

The bulimic woman thus brings to therapy both her pretence of being in charge of her sexuality and the deeper reality of her conflicts, fears and uncertainties. It will often be her first opportunity to confront the complexity of her feelings and defences around sexuality.

Self-Image

The bulimic woman comes seeking help, but she comes with a very poor and degraded sense of herself. This may not be immediately obvious, but it is in fact one of the reasons why women are often so reluctant to come. She has a guilty and horrible secret, which she both wants to share and to cover up. She has no real expectation that when anyone knows what she does they will offer her anything other than condemnation and blame. This, she feels, is what she really deserves. At the Women's Therapy Centre, which has a reputation for working with bulimia, women feel able to present their symptom as a major problem. However, a number of women have told us of being in therapy elsewhere for a number of years and never actually feeling able to 'confess' to being bulimic, for fear of being condemned and rejected.

Alongside this very poor self-image there is, paradoxically, a striving for perfection. Many women have unrealistically high expectations of themselves and of others and a tendency to write off anything which is less than perfect. A dichotomy occurs whereby everything which isn't perfect is experienced as a complete failure. This includes herself ('I ate more of the salad than I meant to so I thought what the hell – I might as well binge and throw it all up'), but also her therapist, who will often find herself rejected if she falls beneath perfection.

Needs

Finally, and most crucially, the bulimic woman brings to therapy all her needs and neediness and her painful emotional conflicts about them. On the one hand, she has a huge sense of being needy, of wanting a great deal from the therapist or group. On the other hand, she believes her needs to be ugly, repulsive and unacceptable and expects to be rejected if she lets them be seen. Again, she wants to demand all the therapist's time, attention and skill but at the same time feels guilty at asking for anything. Here once more the therapist needs to be clear about exactly what is on offer in terms of time and frequency of sessions. The woman needs to know clearly that she can have what is on offer, all of it, and that she need not fear that the therapist will be overwhelmed by her demands and needs.

Group or Individual Therapy?

A one-to-one relationship with a therapist is a very different experience for a woman to being a member of a therapy group. Both can be extremely valuable experiences and both are certainly effective in helping women to understand and overcome the symptom of bulimia. However, some women can best use one method of help, some the other, while others again have found both helpful.

Group therapy works by a number of women jointly sharing their experiences both about bulimia and about any other painful and difficult areas of their lives. This is initially frightening, and women need a certain degree of self-confidence in order to take the step. However, once taken, it can feel enormously reassuring to listen to others and find that you are not alone with your problem.

Both group and individual therapy offer opportunities to talk about relationships and to experience them in the present. In the group, women can experience and learn from the patterns of relationships they form with each other. The group is a microcosm in which relationships can be studied and looked at. A group can be an important place for a woman to learn about the impact of her behaviour on other people. In individual therapy, the relationship between the client and the therapist is often experienced very intensely and will contain some of the elements of the relationship between the woman and her early care-takers.

In one-to-one therapy, the woman has the undivided attention of the therapist during the session. There is less of a sense of competition and less reason to negotiate for time, space and attention. However, for women who often feel terribly deprived and needy, the experience of negotiating time, of learning to ask for something in the group can be a valuable experience.

In both group and individual therapy, the aims are

the same: to enable the woman to translate her symbolic behaviour into terms which reveal the real messages about her life, and to work through the implications of what she discovers. She will use the group and the therapist both to challenge her patterns of behaviour and to support her efforts to change.

Any therapy will help the woman to burst the bubble of bulimia, to move from a situation in which all the bad, difficult, messy feelings in her life are contained by the bulimia. If all goes well, she will move to a position where, like most human beings, she carries a combination of 'good' and 'bad' feelings in all areas of her life and aspects of her personality.

REFERENCES

1. For a more detailed account of the ways in which boundaries play a part in eating disorders, see Mira Dana's chapter, 'Boundaries: One-Way Mirror to the Self', in Marilyn Lawrence (ed), *Fed Up and Hungry*, The Women's Press, London, 1987.
2. See Annie Fursland's 'Eve Was Framed: Food, Sex and Women's Shame', in *Fed Up and Hungry*, *op. cit.*, for a more detailed study of women's sexuality and its links with eating and food.
3. For a more complete account of feminist psychotherapy, see Eichenbaum, L. and Orbach, S., *Understanding Women*, Penguin, Harmondsworth, 1983.

CHAPTER 9

Individual and Group Psychotherapy

In this chapter we go on to offer more detailed accounts of group and individual therapy. We give many examples of the process of each and of the interpretations which we found useful. These comments and interventions of ours are, of course, specific to those particular situations. They should not be taken as either standard comments, which should always be made, nor as the only possible helpful ways of responding. We share them to illustrate the ways in which we work and also to demystify the processes we are describing.

Individual Therapy

The bulimic woman comes to therapy seeking help with her symptom. She will come in desperation about her eating patterns and not able to acknowledge fully that she may have other issues in her life she may need help with. Initially, most of the attention in the therapy will be devoted to her bulimia. Sometimes the therapist may be the first or only person in her world who knows about it, with whom she can talk about it freely. She will certainly need some time just to 'get things off her chest'. This first period will be spent talking about food, her binges and how horrible and disgusting she feels about what she does.

This stage of the therapy should not last too long. The aim of the therapist or counsellor is to help her to move away from this constant and complete concentration on food and eating as the only difficult area in her life. By allowing her to remain stuck talking about the bulimia, the therapist would be colluding with what she herself does — diverting attention from the more painful and serious feelings and conflicts in her life. Of course, her eating patterns must never be ignored. As such a significant symbol, the way she deals with nourishing herself will give both therapist and client vital clues as to what is going on in her inner world. If she neglects to talk about the bulimia at all, the therapist will in effect be doing what the woman herself does: treating her eating pattern as a nasty secret. There therefore needs to be a balance between talking about it and not making it the sole subject of the session.

By moving away from food as the *only* problem, she is able to see her life as a whole and in a more realistic way. Her eating disorder then becomes part of her world, rather than the centre of it; one expression of the 'negative' aspects of herself, rather than the encapsulation of all her badness, her incompetence and self-hatred. For the woman whose symptom is bulimia, therapy itself presents a particular set of contradictions. Because of her difficulty in taking in and keeping in anything good, because of her tendency to experience nourishment as bad and poisonous once she has taken it in, the bulimic woman will have difficulty in taking in anything good from the therapist.

Much as she might want care, attention and support from the therapist and even though she might be able to let herself have it at the time, when the session is over she often tends to get rid of everything she has taken, telling herself that really the therapy is no good, two hours a week isn't enough, so why bother? Or that just talking about things can't really make up for everything that has happened in the past.

We have heard reports from women whose therapists seem to have made interpretations which imply that they really are too greedy, too demanding, thus confirming all their fears. Whether or not the therapists meant their comments to be taken in this way, it is very important not to create this impression. Sometimes the woman herself will project on to her therapist her own sense of guilt at how needy she feels and will experience a rejection which is not there. It is important for the therapist to be on the look-out for this, and to point out to the woman what she is doing if it should happen. If a bulimic woman is allowed to go away with the impression that her therapist rejects her needs and demands, she may well be unable to come back.

The very ambivalent feelings which the woman brings about her own needs must be made explicit and talked about very early on in the therapy. It is in her relationship with the therapist that the woman will begin to allow herself to have her tangle of conflicting feelings. She will experience her love and her hate, wanting to gobble up, to vomit on, wanting to be fed, yet being terrified of the food. There are all kinds of ways to work with a woman on her ambivalence. Sometimes she will express it through her speech, by making a statement and then contradicting it. She expresses it by her pattern of eating and she will express it in the way she responds to the therapy.

Bulimia is very much about unexpressed aggression. This also needs to find expression in the therapy. Bulimia is a very angry symptom. Therapy allows the woman, for the first time, to express her anger in a safe and secure situation, without fear of retaliation. She can express her feelings in words rather than through her eating. If her anger cannot be talked about, it will be acted out in the form of missed sessions, coming late and in general trying to challenge the boundaries of the therapy. It is important to remember that bulimic women are terrified of their aggression and believe they will be rejected for it. It is essential for the therapist to feel supported in withstanding the aggression, talking to the woman about it and maintaining an accepting and understanding attitude. It is easy to get locked into a dynamic whereby the therapist feels vomited on in the sessions and has a sense of inadequacy and impotence. These are feelings which are hard to cope with but which reflect the woman's own sense of inadequacy and her inability to have both loving and angry feelings towards the therapist. It can be difficult for the therapist to hold on to her own sense of value in the face of such attacks and sessions with her supervisor can be vital for her to express and explore her own feelings and discuss the conduct of the therapy in the light of a full understanding of the problem.

Therapy Groups

Group therapy is a process of working on important issues for the individual within the context of a group.

These groups are led by a facilitator or therapist and are thus quite different from the leaderless self-help groups which we will be describing in the next chapter.

In this account of the therapy groups for bulimic women which have been developed at the Women's Therapy Centre, we will go into some of the practical details involved in setting up groups as well as looking at the process of the groups themselves. We do this in an attempt to share our experience with other workers who may themselves be interested in setting up such groups. It is impossible to put into words a process which is as complex and intangible as a therapy group. So much 'goes on' at the conscious and unconscious levels. We do not attempt to describe even a small part of this. Instead, we focus on practical considerations, giving a few examples to provide a taste of what a group can be like.

Starting a Group

The groups which we have found to be most appropriate are year-long groups, of six to eight women, meeting weekly for an hour and a half. We run these groups along analytic lines. Just what we mean by this will become apparent later. We have found it most useful to offer groups in which all the women suffer from the symptoms of bulimia.

Before being invited to join a group, women are seen for an interview with whoever will be leading the group. At this stage we are trying to assess whether a group is the best option for the particular woman and whether she will 'fit' in to the particular group. It also gives us the opportunity to discuss with her practicalities, like times, money and of course commitment.

The profound ambivalence which bulimic women

have towards help and treatment is obvious even at this stage in the process. Many women who contact the Centre in desperation fail to turn up for an interview for a group. They may then phone again, full of apologies, be offered another appointment and again fail to come.

In order to make sense of this contradictory and very irritating pattern of behaviour, we have to understand the investment which the woman has in maintaining her symptom as well as how much she wants to give it up. We have to keep reminding ourselves that her bulimia is the rubbish bin into which she can dispose of all the unwanted and disliked parts of herself. However much she loathes the symptom, she will not give that up without a struggle! The practical fact remains that in order to set up a group, the would-be leader or leaders may have to put aside quite a lot of frustrating hours of missed interviews.

The Initial Interview

In the initial interview, we ask women about most aspects of their lives. Obviously there is some talk about the symptom, the bulimia. We are interested in how serious the symptom is, how preoccupied she is with it and whether it is complicated by addictions to drugs or alcohol. This is not because we want to exclude women who have many difficulties and complicating features in their lives, but because we do need to put together a group which is able to work together. We would therefore prefer not to have a group where all the women have serious addictions in addition to their bulimia. We would prefer that the group did not have to contain unacceptably high levels of anxiety right from the start. We ask about present life circumstances, work, family and background. As with any group, we try not to begin with any one woman feeling isolated or excluded. For example, we would think carefully about taking a woman aged fifty in a group where all the other members were in their twenties, or vice versa.

At the initial interview, we talk about the ambivalence involved in coming to a group and giving up the symptom. We talk about the difficult and painful emotions which can be aroused by being in a group and how important it is that she keeps on coming and talking about those feelings.

At this stage, we also lay down certain 'rules' or boundaries for the group. These are very simple.

1. *Commitment* It is important that she comes to every meeting of the group, and that she comes on time. If for any reason she is unable to come, she should phone and leave a message so that the group knows who is coming and who is not. We make it clear at this stage that the contract with us is for a year. Many bulimic women never commit themselves to anything for so long, and feel relieved and excited about being required to do so.

2. *Money* As the Women's Therapy Centre is a charity, women who can afford to make a financial contribution are asked to do so. We tell them the sliding scale of charges and tell them that if they pay, we would prefer them to pay monthly in advance.

3. *Relationships with Other Members* We ask members of a group not to meet with each other outside the group. This is quite different from a self-help group, where we would encourage women to support each other between sessions. We explain the reasons for this request, that we want all the feelings, issues and conflicts

—

to be contained within the boundaries of the group rather than being taken and 'dealt' with outside. We make it clear that any meetings or contacts which do take place outside the group we regard as 'group business' and the legitimate concern of all members.

This request for boundaries initially puzzles some women and makes them feel angry and frustrated – as though we are trying to control them outside the group. This may have to be discussed at length once the group begins.

We also tell the woman a little about how we will lead the group; that it will not be a structured group, with exercises and suggestions from the leader. Rather, the space will be there for women to use as they want.

At the end of the interview, we tell the woman how and when we will let her know whether we can offer her a place in a group. If we are not able to offer her a place, we will normally offer to see her again to discuss alternative options.

Having interviewed enough women to make up a group of between six and eight it only remains to set a date to begin.

The Aims and Methods of the Groups

The aim of the group as we see it, rather than just to 'get rid' of the bulimia, is to help the woman to reach a stronger position where she has choices. She needs to gain an understanding and insight into what the symptom means in her life, her investment in being bulimic and how she would have to change to give it up.

At another level, the group can provide the opportunity for her to change. One of the most important sources of material for the group is the relationships which are set up between the women in the group and with the therapist. The bulimic woman's assumptions about relationships, about how other people relate to her and how she relates to other people are expressed and reflected in the way she relates to the other members of the group.

The roles of the therapist in the group could be described as administration, containing, analysing.

Administration

As the organizers of the group, we take responsibility for providing the space – which means making sure that the same room is available at the same time each week, providing the creche, if appropriate, and setting the dates. It also means that we mediate between the group and the organization in which the group takes place, for example by establishing and collecting fees.

Containing

This is represented by the fact that we are there every session, providing safety and consistency. We are able and willing to talk about anything which needs to be said. Part of the containing role is to be there on time, to make sure that the group ends on time, even if a member chooses to bring up something very important right near the end. (It often happens that a woman will do this. She wants to talk about something, but because she is so frightened, will make sure that she doesn't actually have time to work on it. Our role is to explain what has happened and then to end the group on time.)

As 'containers', we do not normally talk about our own feelings. Our task is to understand and accept the group's feelings, particularly those feelings which the women themselves find hard to understand and accept.

We can, however, often make use of our own feelings to tell us what is happening in the group. For example, when we were running a group together, one of us always felt very positive and optimistic about the group, while the other had more negative feelings. We came to understand that our split feelings reflected the splitting between the good and bad feelings which is so characteristic of bulimia.

Often in the group the leader will get a sense of impotence, of not giving enough, not being good enough. When we explore these feelings of ours in supervision it becomes clear that the group, full of feelings of desperation and fear and terrified and angry that no one can help, is making us feel this way.

Again, on one occasion the leader continually came away from sessions feeling edgy and churned up. When considering the material from the group it seemed that while the group had been talking about difficult and painful feelings, it had been doing so in a detached and intellectual way, leaving the feelings to the leader.

Analysing
The analysing role is the most complex one. In the kind of groups we are describing, analysis can be made at a number of different levels.

1. The here and now; the relationships in the group between the members. Or the feelings of the whole group.
2. The past; the individual within her own family.
3. Patterns in the relationships of the individuals.

4. The symbolic; the woman's relationship to food and bulimia.
5. Her feelings about herself.
6. Relationship to the therapist.
7. The social; what it means to be a woman.

At different times in the group we will select different levels at which to intervene or offer an interpretation.

Here are some examples from the groups.

A woman talks about her painful relationship with her boyfriend, who gives her a hard time. He makes her wait for him and takes little account of her feelings. This is a relationship which has been going on for years; she keeps 'forgiving' him, keeps allowing him to mess her around. She keeps believing and hoping that he will change one day and stop disappointing her.

In the group, she talks about an event which occurred that week. 'He promised to be there on Friday night so that we could go out together.' But instead of arriving at eight o'clock, he did not come until eleven. He sat for an hour watching television. When she tried to talk to him, to tell him how she felt, he got up and left. In the group, we explore with her how she felt when he came late, didn't want to talk and left. The group helps her to look at why she wasn't able to tell him about her anger, disappointment and feelings of rejection. We connect it with the way in which her mother was very unpredictable and inconsistent. She left her little daughter not only to look after herself, but her brothers and sisters as well. She had the same feelings of anger, disappointment and pain as she experiences now with her boyfriend. We also look at how the bulimia, the taking in and then rejecting of goodness, food, mother, is a reflection of the feelings of anger and disappointment with the person who is not there when needed.

Another woman talks about her boyfriend who has an affectionate name for her – he calls her 'my little hippo'. She feels hurt by this, as she is sensitive about her size, but is not able to confront him with her hurt and anger. Here, we can look at what is happening at the personal level of what it touches in her which is both so painful and yet so paralysing. At the same time, the issue needs a social analysis. Most women would be hurt to be called a hippo! Most women have some difficult feelings about their bodies, and 'hippo' is not normally regarded as a complimentary term.

Interpretations at this social level are often made by members of the group themselves. Often they get angry on each other's behalf and thus help each other to get in touch with the anger which feels so bad and forbidden.

Here is an example of an extract from a group session which will clarify some of these issues.

Lorna says that she no longer has to overeat and make herself sick. Sara: I am fed up with talking about feelings and not actually feeling anything. Apart from Sabina, everyone in this group just intellectualizes. Sabina is the only one who is really in touch with her feelings.

Lorna and Sara now get into an angry exchange in which Sara says she thinks she is in touch with her feelings.

What feelings are these two women evoking in each other? Feelings they don't want to acknowledge in themselves? Perhaps the envy which Lorna's remark provoked, the competitiveness about 'getting better'. This interpretation precipitates two other women bursting into tears, saying they are so embarrassed by the nasty feelings they felt towards Lorna for getting better.

Lorna now starts to undermine her own statement, saying that perhaps she will get worse again. As a bulimic woman she finds it very difficult to be 'OK', to feel different and better than the rest of the group without needing to appease them. Another interpretation is needed both to legitimate and support Lorna in her improvement and also to allow the feelings of the other women, their sense of envy and sadness, perhaps, at not getting better themselves.

Many of the important issues for bulimic women come up around boundaries, in connection with the actual limitations imposed by the groups.

An example: one woman in a bulimia group persistently comes very late. She clearly wants to remain part of the group and expresses a great need for it. But still she comes late. The therapist suggests that the problem may be her ambivalence, her fear of showing her real needs and feelings in the group. This is all accepted. But still she comes late. It is only when an interpretation is made which links her behaviour in the group with her bulimia that she is actually able to feel what she is doing. The therapist suggests that with food, she will order a large meal, but only allow herself to eat part of it. She buys large quantities of food in the supermarket, yet only a very small part of it can be used as nourishing. In the same way, she says, 'yes' to one and a half hours of therapy a week, but cannot allow herself to really have the whole group as a nourishing experience.

The links between the way the woman uses the group and the way she uses her food can also be seen in the tendency of bulimic women to want all or nothing.

Many women in the groups speak of the difficulties they have with the limitations imposed by the group. How can one and a half hours a week possibly be enough? Surely nothing can be accomplished in just a year? Sometimes the anger with the limitations imposed by the group are expressed in less obvious ways: missing sessions, coming but in one way or another not really using the group. Our work with bulimic women aims to help them to begin to realize that getting even some nourishment can be a fulfilling and good experience — even if it does not bring life-long satisfaction! Of course, this doesn't mean that women have to feel content with the little they have. But it does mean that a limited amount of something good is just that. There is something in between all and nothing.

By talking about her frustration with not having everything, rather than just having nothing and saying nothing, the woman gains a sense of deserving something, of being entitled to demand what she wants and to be angry at not getting it. The parallel with the eating behaviour is obvious. She begins by trying to take in everything, all at once, much more than she can manage, and ends up empty, having got rid of it all. In relationships with others, she will search for an intense relationship in which she will have the other person all the time, every minute, caring, nourishing, being there for her. If she cannot have this, she will keep her distance, feel intense disappointment and that she is getting nothing from the relationship at all. It is in making the connection between these different levels of meaning that the real power of group therapy lies.

Another very important issue, which can often be explored via the boundaries of the group, is anger.

In one of the groups, a woman became very upset. It

was shortly before the end of the session and she was in tears, expressing her upset and desperate feelings. When the end of the session came and the group ended another member stayed with her to comfort her. They talked for a long time, and eventually exchanged phone numbers. This happened about two months before the end of the group and they did not tell the group the following week what they had done. A few weeks later, Eleanor announced that she was going to break the rules of the group. She was leaving the country after the group finished and as it had become such an important part of her life she wanted everyone to come to her farewell party. Her only regret was that she knew the therapist would not come.

Following this discussion, Amanda said that she had broken the rules altogether some weeks before with Cynthia. She felt naughty, excited and guilty. When we explored what she was trying to say to the therapist by her actions, she said that she did not want her rules, she wanted to break them. With the end of the group approaching, the therapist was perceived as very powerful, being able to dictate when the group should finish. It had not been long enough. What the therapist was providing was not enough. She wanted to take more than the rules allowed, to tell the therapist to stuff the rules. Along with the anger was despair that anything at all could be achieved.

At that moment, Cynthia said that she was furious. She was encouraged to express and explore her anger. She began to cry, her body shaking, curled up with her face in her hands. 'I love you so much,' she said to the therapist, 'and yet I really hate you. No I don't. But I do. And yet I love you. But I don't. I hate you. How have I ended up feeling like this?'

The therapist pointed out that she was struggling with something that was an issue for everyone in the group. Love and hate; anger and need; hope and despair. These intense ambivalent feelings, so difficult to contain and encompass, are actually a part of human nature. But they are exactly the feelings which bulimia is 'designed' to keep separate and apart from each other.

Ending the Group

The ending of the group is one of its most important phases. If the ending feels complete, if it has been properly acknowledged and the whole gamut of feelings about it expressed, then the group has been a worthwhile experience.

It is important to begin quite early on in the life of the group to talk about the fact that the group is time-limited and will come to an end. The end of the group is one of its most constant themes with issues of control, anger, fear, powerlessness and despair raised in connection with it. As the group progresses, the sense of the impending end increases and so does the intensity of feelings about it. Two months or so before the end of the group, it begins to feel more and more like a pressure cooker. Feelings run high; hurt, despair, disappointment with the therapist, terror of the aloneness which will follow the group are all there. They must all be talked about openly and honestly. The therapist's job is to encourage and validate the verbal expression of feelings about the ending of the group. Bulimic women need the chance to express their despair, their anger about being deserted, to feel that they are entitled to be angry and to be given a space to express it.

The ending is not easy for the therapist either; as well as losing the group she has come to care about, she has heard the group telling her angrily about what they haven't got from it, their fears for what lies ahead and how they love and hate her for what she has and hasn't given them.

CHAPTER 10

Self-Help

This chapter is written specifically for bulimic women who are interested in the possibilities of forming a self-help group. At the Women's Therapy Centre, as well as developing ways of working with bulimic women in individual therapy and group therapy, we have also pioneered the setting-up of self-help groups. The Centre has recently offered short-term workshops of two days for a group of up to ten women who then meet and work as a self-help group. These groups have been extremely helpful to some women. The following suggestions and guidelines are based both on our experience of them and on a booklet written by the authors, 'Guidelines for Bulimia Self-Help Groups', copies of which are available from the Women's Therapy Centre.

We recognize that many women with the symptom of bulimia are not able to have access to the rather scarce resources of psychotherapy. Often women living in rural areas, away from large towns, simply do not have access to therapy centres or to hospital departments specializing in the treatment of bulimia. For these women, setting up a self-help group can provide a viable alternative source of help. We would not, however, want to imply that self-help is just an inferior substitute for working with a therapist. We have come to understand the enormous strength, support and self-validation which women can derive from working together with other bulimic women. Some women much prefer the idea of working with others who have a similar problem and find this an easier option to consider than help from 'professionals'. A self-help group works without a leader or therapist and so right from the start the women themselves have to take the responsibility for the group. The literature on women's self-help groups suggests that although the process can be difficult, it can also be richly rewarding.

Things to Think About Before a Group Begins

Ambivalence
This ambivalence you feel towards food will be evident in many areas of your life. One of these areas could be your wish to find help and it may sometimes cause you to seek help whilst not really feeling able to use it. When seeking help, it is important to be aware of this. Be prepared for mixed feelings and confused reactions. Don't let this put you off!

Where Do I Start?
Many of the women who have managed to overcome the symptom of bulimia have told us that the first step for them consisted of making a decision to stop vomiting on a certain date, either altogether or for one or two days a week. If you don't feel ready to make such a decision, don't worry. But just bear it in mind.

The Role of Bulimia in Your Life
Try to think of your day-to-day life and place the bulimia within it. Try to understand its connections with the rest of your experience.

Some of the questions you can ask yourself are:

> How much time does it take up?
> Who knows about it?
> How does it feel to have this secret life?
> How many hours a day do you spend at it?
> What would you do with your time if you gave it up?
> Are you afraid of having time for yourself?
> Can you think of any positive things bulimia does for you? (Such as giving you a secret life, letting you feel superior to other women who overeat and get fat, etc.)
> What do you think bulimia might be saying to someone in your life? Think of it as a statement. Who are you saying it to and what are you saying?

Next time you have the urge and the opportunity to overeat and vomit, don't let yourself be panicked into it. Make yourself sit down for at least twenty minutes and think about all the different ways you might spend the time. What would you prefer to do? If you decide to eat and make yourself sick, that is your choice, but at least you have made a decision about it. Nothing outside yourself made you do it.

We do not believe that overeating and vomiting is simply a habit (although it does have a habitual quality to it). It also needs to be understood as a way of expressing distress. When asked, some of the women in the groups said strongly, 'I eat most of the time out of habit. I'm just used to doing it and when I'm bored I go and eat. It's a habit.' When the suggestion was introduced to the groups that eating and vomiting may relate to how the woman is feeling, these women adopted a new perspective and found to their surprise that the meaning of their eating went much deeper than just an habitual activity. Following that understanding, they found connections between their eating and their emotions. Various emotions such as sadness, loneliness, inadequacy, excitement, happiness, etc., seemed to drive them to eating and vomiting.

It might be helpful for you to try to look at your own eating behaviour in the same way and try to discover which experiences seem to evoke it and which ones don't. One way to do this is to sit down at the end of the day and think about how it went. Write down when you overate and made yourself sick. How did you feel before that? What did you eat, how did you feel afterwards?

Another way of doing it is to make a list of when you tend to eat and vomit, and try to find the connections with how you are feeling at these times. For example: 'I often binge and vomit in the evening between about six and seven o'clock.'

What happens at that time?

'This is about the time I come in from work. Typically I will have had a hard day. My boss makes a lot of demands on me. I feel really tired. It is too early to go to sleep. I feel lonely and want to be taken care of. There is no one there. I eat and vomit.'

Or, 'After breakfast the kids leave for school. I'm not hungry, but find myself near the fridge and eating again. I have to make myself sick.'

What do you feel?

'The kids just left. I feel lonely and empty. All I have to do is the housework which I don't want to do, but I feel I have to.'

And so on.

The Physical Effects of Bulimia

Many women who contact us are very concerned about the physical effects which eating and vomiting may cause. If you are at all worried about the physical consequences of your eating disorder, you should consult your doctor or perhaps a local well-woman clinic. If you do not get the advice and information you need, or if you meet with a hostile or dismissive response, ask to be referred to a specialist. This could be an important step towards really beginning to take care of yourself and taking your physical needs seriously.

Self-Help Groups

Maybe now when you have some general ideas about bulimia and some of the possible connections with your own personal life, you would like to try working on your problem in a self-help group. One important thing to remember is that even after some time of working at finding out the feelings, reasons, connections, you may still feel that you have not solved anything. It is very important to be patient, not to expect too much too quickly. Our experience is that it takes a long time and a lot of hard and painful work to get to the core of a problem and to change a symptom which may have been with you for a number of years. Even if you discover the connections, don't be discouraged if things don't move. Themes will come up again and again. You will give up the symptom when you are ready to do so.

How to Set Up a Group

You may know a woman who lives near you and who suffers from the same problem. You could start your group in a very simple way by combining your courage and effort. You might place a notice on a local notice-board or advertise in the local press for women to contact you if they are interested in working in a self-help group on overeating and vomiting. If you do this, be prepared for a big response. An awful lot of women suffer from bulimia!

Write to the national organizations which might have information on existing local groups and resources. (Addresses at the end of this book.)

Get hold of some of the books on eating disorders and self-help. A list, with suggestions on how to begin, is at the end of this chapter.

Some General Principles in Self-Help Groups

Time Sharing

This can be very important in this type of group. Women who think of themselves as 'greedy' might feel very reluctant to take up the group's time. We have also learnt that the women who seem to have least to say may be able to make a very helpful contribution if they are given the opportunity to do so.

It is therefore a good idea to structure the group so that there is an expectation that everyone will say something about a particular theme or issue. On the other hand, it is useful to leave some unstructured time, which can be used by those women who feel that a particular area of work has a special meaning for them.

One way of achieving this is to allocate, for instance, half the time (maybe an hour) to a time-shared theme – sixty minutes divided by the number of women – leaving the second hour for a more general discussion of the issues that arise. It is useful to appoint a time-keeper, who sits with a watch and indicates to women when their time is up. It is good to have a different woman time-keeping at each session so that you share responsibilities as equally as possible.

Meeting Place

It is best for the members of the group to rotate meeting in each others' homes. Ideally the members will live near each other, so that travelling long distances will not become a reason and excuse to leave the group when things become difficult. Hence, rotating meetings in homes in the same area is easy, and is important, especially in order that different women take responsibility at different sessions. In this way no one woman in the group feels that she is the regular 'hostess' of the group.

Themes

It is important to arrange beforehand a theme, exercise or something to work on. This could be done either by preparing a plan for a few sessions in advance, or by leaving a few minutes at the end of every meeting to discuss the plan for the next week. Later on in this chapter, we outline a number of themes which the group might follow.

Social Aspects of the Group

The group should be aware of not allowing the sessions to become a social situation where the members are meeting to chat to each other about the last few days. Here are some rules that may help you.

1. All members make a commitment to come to every session and to come on time.
2. If one woman cannot come to a session, she should notify the group in advance. If something urgent comes up just before the group, she should phone the person in whose house that session is to be held, in order that the rest of the group will not wait for her.
3. The group should start on time exactly and if people want coffee before the group they should come a bit earlier. In this way, the length of the session (2–2½ hours) will be fully used for work.

Confidentiality

In the beginning of the group, the issue of confidentiality must be stressed. Some groups will take place in small towns or villages where people know each other. It is easier to trust the group and to be open if a commitment is made to keep all that happens within the group confidential. Also, try not to discuss the session amongst yourselves if you meet socially between sessions as this will have the effect of excluding other women.

Feelings

It is important for the group to find the capacity to allow women to experience and express uncomfortable feelings. Often when a woman talks about painful feelings and starts to cry, the rest of the women, not knowing what to do, feel uneasy trying to comfort her: 'It will be all right'. We realize that a woman crying could bring uncomfortable feelings for the rest of the group. However, it is very important for the woman to stay with these feelings with the support of the group. As we usually find indirect ways of dealing with these difficult feelings – and one of the ways is by overeating and vomiting – it is vital to be able to express these feelings and not try to comfort them away.

Leaving the Group
Sometimes women who have only been in a group for a few weeks stop overeating and making themselves sick and hence feel they have solved the problem and want to leave the group. It is not impossible for such a thing to happen, but it is important to allow yourself to stay with the group for longer than this as it is highly unlikely that a problem that has been with you for some considerable time will disappear overnight.

The same applies to women who, feeling that they have been in the group for a long time and that nothing has happened, want to give up. It is long, hard work; give yourself time both to gain understanding of your problems and be able to use it to change your behaviour and establish a new pattern for yourself.

The Sessions

The group is set up. You know who is coming, when and where it will take place and for how long. All practical issues have been arranged and we can now begin to think about the content of the sessions.

Every group will have its own themes and issues which will emerge as being 'the important ones' for your group. We can only share with you those which have emerged as important in the groups with which we have been involved. Try being creative with these guidelines and find your group's way of working with them.

1. Why Are We Here?
This session should involve everyone in the group talking about why they are there, how they came to the group, what treatment, if any, they have had and so on. It can be a good way of getting to know each other, who everyone is and why they have come to the group. What women expect from the group should also be talked about.

Remember that some women will never have been in a group or in 'therapy' before, so don't expect too much of each other! You should expect that being able to talk about the very fact that they make themselves sick will be a dramatic and moving experience for some women. Don't press women to say more than they want to at this stage. Women need to be given permission to talk, but also permission to withhold. The first session will probably be mostly taken up by everyone talking as much as they can about the problem they are bringing to the group. The relief that this kind of sharing can bring cannot be overstated. Women are often amazed that everyone else in the group seems so normal and competent. If you spend a number of years considering yourself as a freak, you are bound to be surprised that other women like yourself appear not to be!

2. The Importance of Bulimia in My Life
An attempt to see the importance of bulimia in your life. This can be done both by telling the story of your bulimia

—

– When did it start? What was your life situation at the time? What job did you do? Did you live with anyone at the time? – and by looking at your current life situation in terms of the same kinds of questions.

You can either take some time each to talk about this or if you prefer you can represent your life as a kind of diagram. Take two sheets of paper, one for the time when you began overeating and vomiting, and one for your current situation. Put yourself in the centre of the page, and all the other people, events, jobs – anything you consider important – round the outside. Include wishes, fantasies and aspirations.

Job Part-time secretary		*Husband, Bill* – depressed, unhappy at work
Mother – needing a lot of my time	ME	*Children* – 7 and 9
My women's group – made me feel needy and discontented		*My exercise class* – something for myself
	What I would really like to do – go back to college	

Then think about the bulimia. Who knows about it, how much time does it take up, how does it fit in?

Do the same for when the bulimia started. Look at people, emotions, expectations. Try comparing the two pictures with the help of the group. Find out the important connections.

The question you should focus upon is, 'Where does bulimia fit in with the rest of your life?' You could spend the first half of the group in a time-shared exchange and the remaining time discussing those themes which are common to all or several women.

3. *The Symptom Itself*

Try talking in the most frank and honest way you can manage about the actual symptom of overeating and vomiting. When do you do it? How often? What do you mostly eat? Where do you buy your food? What are your thoughts before doing it? How do you plan the overeating episode? Try going into the details of the planning and overeating as much as possible, with reference to feelings, expectations, wishes. Then try to talk about making yourself sick. How do you do it? Do you use your finger? Are there people around? Do you do it secretly? What do you feel before actually vomiting? And while you are making yourself sick? Do you throw up everything you have eaten? Do you spend much time cleaning up after yourself? How much time does the whole thing take?

The more detail you can share the better it is. You will initially find it embarrassing to share such intimate details of your life, but in our experience it is a great relief to share something you feel so ashamed of with other women who really understand. If you are not able to share the reality of your bulimia with the group you may end up feeling that you have a guilty secret which the group does not know about – and feeling that they would reject you if they knew the truth. Remember that every woman in the group is taking this tremendous risk and that it is a risk worth taking.

4. *Feelings Associated with Bulimia*

This session might be spent considering how bulimia makes you all feel about yourselves.

It makes women feel ashamed, dirty, unfeminine. But also perhaps exhilarated and excited. What else do you have in your life which you don't share with anyone?

You may want to discuss this issue in pairs and then feed back to the large group. You could take ten minutes each to discuss it in pairs and then the rest of the session to discuss common themes and differences amongst you.

Another way of doing it is to write down, 'How bulimia makes me feel about myself'. On one page write the good feelings, on the other, the bad feelings.

5. The Statement

Look at the person who is most predominant in the picture you drew in the second session; what feelings do you have towards them? What expectations? What do you want to say to them that you have never said? Is there a statement that is so important it can never be stated? Remember, this is a group of women who have the same problem as you. They experience the same feelings, so in this environment it is safe to say the things that you could not say to that person – to state the statement. You may start with a simple statement: 'I don't like what you did yesterday . . . actually, coming to think of it, you do it one way or another every day . . . You make me angry . . . You don't give me any respect . . .' You may find yourself going on to make stronger and stronger statements towards the person.

It might make it easier if you talked to a cushion as though it were that person, or if one member of the group sits in front of you as though they were that person in your life. (It could be your mother, husband, boyfriend, girlfriend, etc.) You could explain to the group member (who is now your mother, for example) the character of your mother and the kind of interaction that you have with her, and she could answer accordingly. You would be surprised how precise people can be once they get the character of the person involved. This may also give you another perspective on how the other person (your mother in this example) may feel.

6. *Ambivalence*

As we mentioned earlier, one of the important issues in bulimia is ambivalence. This could be reflected in your life in many different ways. The most obvious way is in the ambivalent attitude towards nourishment.

You may feel an intense craving for nourishment, but be unable to keep it in. Hence, it feels like a constant battle between wanting to take in but not feeling able to have. It is like a battle between agreeing and disagreeing, between yes and no, between consuming and rejecting. In the beginning, to look at this aspect of the problem you could try to find out how ambivalence is expressed in your life. It could be reflected in your way of speaking, for example: 'I do . . . but . . .; I want . . . but . . .; I am happy . . . no, not really . . .' It could be reflected in your behaviour: doing things half-heartedly; or in your attitudes towards people around you, in relationships, etc.

This exploration could take different forms. Try to match it with the ways in which the ambivalence is expressed, such as in the way of speaking. A woman who makes a statement and immediately contradicts herself should try to see how it feels to make one definite statement. For example, if you say, 'He's horrible, unbearable, no, you know what I mean, he's OK in some ways, but . . .' try staying with one statement first: 'He's horrible.' If you cannot do this, try to find out what it is that you fear. What is the feeling that you get when you try to stay with one statement? This could also be done as an exercise within the group, talking about attitudes to the group, to treatment, to people in the group, etc.

Try to be gentle and not use this as an attacking experience, but as one from which you can learn.

7. *Changing*

Changing is sometimes an important theme. Bulimic women have often undergone many changes in their size and shape over the years. The group can share accounts of how their body size has changed and what effects these changes have had on the way they feel about themselves. Often there is a great longing for sameness, for a consistent identity but at the same time a strong will to change the self towards some conception of perfection.

8. *Time and Space*

Time and space can be an important theme and certainly well worth spending some time on. It can be a difficult area to get in to. Try going round the group, asking each woman how she structures time when she is alone. Many bulimic women lead such busy lives that they rarely have to confront the problem of unstructured time. In our experience there can be a great deal of panic at the thought of 'free' time. For some women, the ritualistic process of overeating and making themselves sick helps them to avoid the panic and the decisions about what to do. Bulimia can be experienced as 'time out' – there may be other ways of taking time out!

9. *The Ritual*

It might be worth spending some time on the theme of the bulimic ritual. What exactly do members of the group do? You will find that you mostly do quite similar things. You can also take the rare opportunity to laugh at yourselves. In the past, women have found that it is much more difficult to engage in these ritualistic activities after they have shared them at a group.

10. *The Fear of Being Fat*

Many women with eating problems, even if they look 'normal' or 'slim' to the objective eye, feel fat or overweight. *Fat Is a Feminist Issue*, by Susie Orbach, describes the conscious and unconscious reasons for a woman becoming fat and the protective function this fat may have for her. The fat/thin fantasy (page 75 of *Fat Is a Feminist Issue*) is very helpful for exploring a woman's investment in either being or feeling over-weight. This could be helpful for some of you, and you may want to try working with the fantasy. However, some of you may want to explore your fear of being fat and one way of looking at this issue is again through fantasy work.

The fantasy You are a film-maker. You sit in a cinema all on your own, in front of a table. You have everything you need to write the story and make the film. On the table there are two projectors. On the wall in front of you are two screens. Remember, you are the director and the story writer; it is all in your hands.

On the right-hand screen appears a very thin woman. She is very skinny, and she is walking towards you. She is the heroine of your film and you are creating the story of her life. Who is she? What is her job? What is her family like? Is she married? What is her social life like? Where is she coming from? Where is she going? She now enters her home. What does it look like? Is she with a lover? A husband? What is her sex life like?

Then on the left-hand screen a fat woman appears. Go through the same process with her. Compare in the group the images of the fat woman's life and the thin woman's life which appear in different women's fantasies.

Another exercise: give eight adjectives that come to mind to fit the phrase, 'fat woman', and then give eight adjectives that fit the phrase, 'thin woman'.

11. Relationships with Parents

Relationships with mothers and fathers have emerged as a powerful theme in our groups. This is often a painful area and needs to be approached with great sensitivity. We find that 'deprivation' or the idea of deprivation is an important factor in bulimia. It emerges often as a feeling of having been denied a real understanding and as a withholding of 'good things' from the parents, whilst at the same time parents are felt to be over-controlling and over-intrusive.

You should expect a good deal of anger to be expressed if you decide to devote a session to this theme! Some issues that could be explored are:

> Your mother's and father's ambivalence in their attitudes towards you and your siblings.
> Their inconsistency in attitude and reaction to the family.
> In which ways did you feel deprived as a child?
> What was your mother's attitude to food?
> What was her attitude to her body? Femininity? Sexuality?

What was her attitude to your body? Femininity? Sexuality?

There are many other questions that you could ask concerning this issue and there are many ways of working on it. *In Our Own Hands* by Sheila Ernst and Lucy Goodison is a good source book for ideas and exercises. Try to be creative with this and other sessions.

You could take up two consecutive sessions for this subject and you could come back to it every so often, e.g. after ten sessions on other issues. If you do this, you could divide the subject into specific aspects, such as mother and food, mother and sexuality, parents and anger and so on.

12. Sexuality

It might be useful to spend a session thinking about sexuality. To what extent is sex a problematic issue in your lives? Can you only feel sexual when you are thin? Is sex about meeting your own needs or about proving to other people that you are OK?

The first chapter of *Fed Up and Hungry* will give you some ideas about the relationship between food and sex in women's lives.

13. A Form of Crying

Some women in groups have related to bulimia as another form of crying. This may or may not be true for you. However, if you want to explore this aspect of bulimia in your life, here are some questions which could help you to do this. You could either use them to prepare some thoughts before the session or try developing these within the group as a discussion.

–

What is the crying about?
Is it past or present?
What are the feelings that come with the crying?
Is it a cry of despair? Of pain, anger, anguish?
Who hurt you?
Are you crying for help from someone specific?
From whom do you want comfort?

Try to find out about your own personal crying and what the alternatives are. Are you able to express your feelings in a different way?

14. *The Decision*

You may want to use a session to try to make a decision about stopping vomiting. It can be helpful at this point to talk about decision-making in general for you, before you become more specific about decisions concerning your eating. How do you make decisions? Do you usually find it difficult to make up your mind? How do you feel when you are faced with a number of options and have to choose one of them? Does it take you long to make a decision? How do you feel about the 'lost options' – the ones you did not choose? Do you usually hope that other people or external events will take the decision out of your hands? Try to differentiate between major life decisions which are difficult for anyone, and day-to-day ones, which are harder for some people than for others. *In Our Own Hands* has some good suggestions for exercises in decision-making.

After having discussed the issue in general, you may want to plan how to make a decision about changing your eating pattern, e.g. to stop making yourself sick after meals. You may either want to do this immediately or to plan a gradual change. Some aspects that you could discuss with the group are:

> What are the implications of such a decision in your life?
> What other areas of your life will change?
> Who will you be, if you don't overeat and make yourself sick?
> What will help you to stop?
> What kind of support do you need?
> How can the group help?

15. *Food in My Stomach*

This exercise is designed to look at how it feels to have food in your stomach and what it is that is so disturbing that you have to get rid of it as soon as possible. As with all fantasy work, get as comfortable as you can — try to relax and breathe deeply for a few minutes, then shut your eyes. (You can record it if you like, before the session, leaving long pauses where the dots are.)

The fantasy You are coming back from work . . . you have had a hard day . . . you are feeling very tired . . . you are not very hungry . . . all you want is a bath and a rest . . . however, you are thinking of food . . . you are imagining all the food you are going to buy . . . you are then going into the supermarket . . . you are buying all the food you can eat in one sitting . . . you walk home with the food . . . you start eating . . . you eat as much as you can . . . now stay in the place where you have just eaten . . . try to feel the food in your stomach . . . how does it feel . . . try to get an image of the food inside you . . . any colours? movement? sensation? . . . process of digestion . . . try to get as much information as you can about the feeling of the food in your stomach . . . and when you are ready, open your eyes . . . come back to the group.

Now try to discuss with the group what came up for you in the fantasy.

16. Emotions

Following the assumption that bulimia is not just a habit, and that each time a woman overeats and makes herself sick there are underlying emotions which drive her to such behaviour, it may be useful to look at one occasion when you overate and vomited, and try to analyse it with this understanding in mind.

Doing this in the supportive environment of the group will feel less threatening and may throw some light on the underlying emotions. It could be done either as a fantasy for the whole group (perhaps preparing a tape beforehand) or in pairs, where two listen and help each other work in turn. Each group can create their own fantasy and way of asking questions, but here are some of the things to concentrate on:

> Try doing a relaxation and breathing exercise in the group before you start.
> Close your eyes; try to remember the last time you overate and made yourself sick.
> Try analysing what happened before eating and vomiting. Go back until you get hold of the feeling that may have been connected with this behaviour. Then try and look at what the bulimia did for you in that situation. How did it help you to deal with those feelings?

At the end of the session, each member of the group can look at the situation she described and the feelings involved and look with each other at more direct ways she could have dealt with these feelings. (E.g. if loneliness was what she felt drove her to eating and vomiting, what could she otherwise have done about her loneliness? If it was anger, how could she deal with her anger in a more direct way?)

17. *The Secret*

As we have already explained, the secrecy of bulimia is an important aspect of it in a number of ways. In this session, you may want to start looking at it and what it means for you. You could start by having an imaginary conversation (in the session with the help of the group), with the person you feel closest to. A conversation, in which you are telling them about your bulimia, in a lengthy and detailed way. Tell them what you do, how often, how long you have been overeating and making yourself sick, how you feel when doing it, after having done it, and so on.

Each woman will ask another woman in the group to sit in front of her, and to be the person in her life to whom she wants to tell the secret. Now we would like you to think: Who is the person who first comes to mind when you think of whom you would most like to tell the secret to? What reaction do you expect? Who is the person you are most afraid to tell this to? What is the reason for this fear? What reaction do you expect? What reaction would you like from this person? Can you express this wish in the imaginary conversation you are having with them? (For example, 'You know I'm so afraid that you won't talk to me any more. I would so

like you to understand, to hold me, tell me you love me
and accept me . . .')

18. *Body Image*

Many women described themselves as fat and unattractive after a big meal, and acceptable or OK if they did
not eat or after having vomited. In this session you
might like to explore body image and how it changes.
One good way to do this is through drawing. We
suggest that you draw yourself (on separate pages) 1.
before a binge; 2. after a binge; 3. after making yourself
sick. Take about seven minutes for each drawing and
remember that the artistic quality of the picture does
not matter at all. Do the drawings before you read any
further. Now try to concentrate individually on the
pictures that you have just done, and compare them.
Some guidelines for what to look at; see how old the
person in each picture looks. Where does the emphasis
lie? On the eyes? . . . hands? . . . on the stomach? What
is the expression on the face in each of them? Are there
any parts of the face or body missing? Which? What
does it mean? (For example, what does it mean for a
woman to draw herself with no hands? What do hands
do? What do they symbolize for her?)

Now try looking at the page as your space. See how
much of your space you have actually used in the
drawing. Is there enough space? Too much? Do you fill
the page or are you a small part of it? Is there a
difference between the amount of space you take up
before and after a binge? Before and after making
yourself sick? Try to compare the three drawings carefully; pay attention to the differences and to the meaning of these differences. You can learn a great deal from

this exercise by paying attention to the details and their meanings.

19. *Word Associations*
Sometimes, in order to find out connections and feelings about a certain event or action, word association can be helpful and revealing. There are several words you could try this exercise with. You could do it as a group exercise, where the whole group makes a list of associations, like a brainstorm. Or by each member writing down her own associations. Try not to think too hard before you write down or say the associations. Then together with the group you can look at the feelings these words carry. For this exercise you can choose relevant words for your own situation. Some of our suggestions are: vomit, fat, food, sick, thin, eating.

20. *Needs*
One of the very important issues when working in a group on bulimia is the ambivalence and conflict around needs. Feeling needs, allowing oneself to actually feel the need and to express it to the person it involves, is a very difficult thing for a woman to do.

Obviously, when you turn to food, overeat and make yourself sick there is something which you need which you are either unaware of or unable to express. So the first thing for each member of the group to do is to recognize that not only does she have needs (like all human beings) but that she must learn slowly to listen and attend to them. This includes needs on all levels: physical, emotional, intellectual. This could be done by each member of the group exploring her fantasy about what would happen if she needed something or someone. How she might be abused if she expressed needs, or about what would happen to others if she needed them.

On another level, a fantasy about early experiences with parents may be tried. Go back to any age in your childhood ... you are afraid ... you need someone to hold you ... you go to your mother, ask for a cuddle ... What is her reaction? Does she cuddle you? What does she say? What does she do?

Another way of doing this is for someone to role-play mother or father, in order to explore the reaction – such as anger, acceptance, hesitance, silence, rejection, etc. – that the woman faced as a child when she asked for something.

REFERENCES

1. See for example, Noble, K., 'Self Help Groups – The Agony and the Ecstasy', in Lawrence, M. (ed), *Fed Up and Hungry*, The Women's press, London, 1987.

Useful Books for Self-Help Groups

Boskind-White, M., and White, W. C., *Bulimarexia,* Norton, New York, 1983.

Ernst, Sheila, and Goodison, Lucy, *In Our Own Hands*, The Women's Press, London, 1981.

Lawrence, Marilyn, *The Anorexic Experience*, The Women's Press, London, 1984.

Lawrence, Marilyn, *Fed up and Hungry*, The Women's Press, London, 1987.

Orbach, Susie, *Fat is a Feminist Issue*, Hamlyn, London, 1979.

Orbach, Susie, *Fat is a Feminist Issue 2*, Hamlyn, London, 1984.

CHAPTER 11

Final Thoughts

In this book we have tried to present and analyse bulimia in as broad a context as possible. The more perspectives and levels of understanding we can offer, the more, we hope, women and their helpers will be able to identify with and use our work.

We have been particularly concerned to understand the individual within the context of both her family and the wider society. Much of the existing theory and practice concerned with eating disorders fails to take the interaction of these different contexts into account. Some consider only the individual, as a 'person', locked into her miserable world. This approach fails to see the sufferer as a woman, sharing with other women the constraints and limitations of stereotypes and social roles. Other accounts look at the individual within the context of his or her family, seeing the family as the focus of the distress and thus the target for treatment. Such an account can leave the individual's situation unattended to and falls short of providing a full picture of families as part of the social world. It is the shortcomings of these approaches which so often leave bulimic women and their families feeling misunderstood.

We began our exploration by posing the vital questions, Why women? Why food? Why now? and Why bulimia? The book itself is not merely an answer to these questions, but an attempt to analyse, describe and provide an understanding of the bulimic woman's life.

The ways in which women use their bodies as a major arena in which to exert some control over a life which is often experienced as out of control is only one of the issues to do with gender which we suggest determines the symptom of bulimia. The conflict centring on the body as both her most valuable commodity on the one hand and her most shameful and imperfect feature on the other is an intense one for many women. Equally important in the reality of most women's lives is the need to care for others, to put her own needs second, which leads to a powerful sense of not deserving and a wish to deny and eradicate her own needs and feelings. Little wonder that many women develop a wish to become 'perfect', superwomen, cut off from all need, messiness and their own physical selves. It is this gap between the external realities of life and women's internal feelings which can be so destructive.

We are not, of course, suggesting that women are merely the passive victims of society's demands and contradictions. We are particularly interested in the ways in which women internalize social processes and create an inner world which reflects them. We also understand bulimia as an angry, aggressive symptom, a silent and secret way of not conforming.

It is the secrecy of the symptom which provides us with much of the information about its nature and meaning. The secret symptom of bulimia represents and contains the woman's fear of chaos and disorder, her sense of her own badness and madness which is kept separate and apart from the rest of her well-ordered life.

Since bulimia is precisely about 'coping', carrying on with life and never openly expressing distress, invocations to 'pull yourself together' are so damaging to the woman with bulimia. This is the exact phrase she uses herself, every morning when she wakes up, every night before she goes to sleep and many times in between. It is her ability to do just this, to maintain a façade of competence and coping which perpetuates her symptom.

Doctors, as sympathetic as they may sometimes want to be, rarely have the time or the understanding of the woman who presents herself with her symptom to see that it is not helpful to collude with her attempts to 'pull herself together'.

Families and friends are frequently sympathetic and helpful for quite a long time, but often, sooner or later, patience wears thin and they too, either openly or non-verbally, give the woman the message to 'pull herself together'. Bulimia is, of course, an enormously difficult and frustrating symptom for families and friends to have to live with. To see someone you care for engaged in such a seemingly futile and painfully destructive cycle eventually produces an angry and dismissive response. The bulimic woman's pattern is to take in, but ultimately to reject not only her food, but all the help and concern they can offer too.

It is our hope that having read this book, bulimic women, their families, friends and doctors will no longer think that 'pull yourself together' is a useful response.

So what would a more helpful response amount to? What does the bulimic woman need in order to be able to move forward towards a way out of the trap she finds herself in? To sum it up, we would say that she needs two things: understanding and choice.

Understanding from friends and family who know about the woman's difficulties amounts to an acceptance of the frustrating and destructive symptoms as signs of distress rather than a bad habit. The symptom of bulimia, because it is such an aggressive and rejecting symptom, can often feel like a personal attack. Mothers in particular and domestic partners often do feel attacked by the symptom, as though it is a silent rejection and rebuke. This can make them feel even more impotent and guilty and can actually result in them behaving in rejecting ways. Of course, the symptom may contain a message to important people in the bulimic woman's life, but in our experience there is little point in those people adopting a guilty and defensive stance. Much better for them to express their feelings openly and to encourage the bulimic woman to do the same. After all, one of her central problems is her need to appease and always appear as though everything is all right. We have looked at how important it is for the bulimic woman herself to develop a sense of her own boundaries, within which she can take account of her own needs; it is also important for those who are close to her to be able to do the same, even if this sometimes means saying 'no' to her, whilst maintaining a basically sympathetic attitude. It is perfectly possible to understand the pain and distress which underlie the perplexing and frustrating symptom of bulimia, whilst saying that at the moment one isn't able to offer any more help. Much better this than an endless and fruitless battle over the symptom.

For the bulimic woman herself, understanding amounts to an attempt to get to the bottom of what the symptom means for her, in her own life, past and present, and to discover the nature of the conflicts which push her into this way of coping. To begin with, if you are suffering from the symptom of bulimia, you must try to think of it as an outward sign of some hidden distress. It is not a disgusting and monstrous part of you which emerges from nowhere; it does not represent a dangerous part of you which will consume everyone around you, or make them disappear full of horror and contempt. What it does represent is the needy and infantile part of you, which you want to conceal and deny. Asking for help may well be the most difficult thing you have ever done and you will have gathered from reading this book that the process of recovery will not be an easy one. You may well find that very vulnerable and frightening feelings which have been hidden and almost forgotten come to the fore and that you find yourself feeling more confused, angry and upset than you are used to feeling. On the positive side, we have never met anyone who has given up the symptom of bulimia who is not very pleased to be rid of it.

This brings us to the second important thing the bulimic woman needs: choice. Choice implies respect and permission. It is extremely important that bulimia is seen for what it is: a way of coping. It is not a self-indulgence or a sign of weakness but rather a mechanism for dealing with life's difficulties. It has been adopted in a desperate attempt to keep going – and in a very limited and self-punishing way, it works. In our experience, it is absolutely vital to respect the way a woman has tried to handle her situation, whilst acknowledging that there might be better ways.

In our work at the Women's Therapy Centre, one of

the ways in which we try to ensure that women really are exercising choice is by insisting that they refer themselves. However desperate she might feel, she still has to make up her own mind about when she is ready to tackle her symptom. Very often the first approach to us is made by a friend or relative and while we are happy to talk with them about their own worries and concerns about the woman's problem, it is the woman herself who must ask for what she wants.

When someone joins a group or comes to a workshop at the Centre we do not tell her when or how to give up her symptom. Again, she must be in charge of the timing and we do not believe it will help her to feel controlled or constrained. As we see our own role, it is in terms of providing space for her to reach her own self-understanding and therefore be in a stronger position to make her own choices.

In this book we have not minimized or understated the problem of bulimia. We have tried to present the facts honestly and our own analysis of the underlying issues which we take very seriously. But we do have an essentially optimistic attitude to eating disorders. Of course it is our hope that gradually social processes will change, that our society will begin to realize the absurdity of its expectations for women and that in time girls will be brought up to value themselves in quite a different way. In the meantime it is vitally important for women who already suffer from eating disorders to find the sympathetic space that they need to begin to explore and resolve their difficulties.

RESURCES

·

UK
Anorexic Aid,
The Priory Centre,
11 Priory Road,
High Wycombe,
Bucks

Anorexic Family Aid,
Sackville Place,
44 Magdalen Street,
Norwich,
Norfolk

The Women's Therapy Centre,
6 Manor Gardens,
London N7

USA
The Women's Therapy Centre Institute,
80 East 11th St,
New York, New York 10003

NORWAY
Interessegruppa for kvinner med spiseforstyurrelser,
Box 9917 1LA,
0132 Oslo

HOLLAND
Stichting Eetverslaving,
postbus 43075,
1009 ZB Amsterdam

SUGGESTED FURTHER READING

Boskind-Lodahl, M., 'Cinderella's Stepsisters: A Feminist Perspective on Anorexia and Bulimia', *Signs: Journal of Women in Culture and Society*, 1976, 2, 342–56.

Boskind-White, M., and White, W. C., *Bulimiarexia, The Binge/Purge Cycle*, Norton, New York, 1983.

Bruch, H., *Eating Disorders*, Routledge & Kegan Paul, London, 1974.

Chasseguet-Smirgel, J., *Creativity and Perversion*, Free Association Books, London, 1985.

Chernin, K., *Womansize. The Tyranny of Slenderness*, The Women's Press, London, 1983.

Chernin, K., *The Hungry Self*, Virago, London, 1986.

Coward, R., *Female Desire*, Paladin, London, 1984.

Crisp, A. H., *Anorexia Nervosa: Let Me Be*, Academic Press, London, 1980.

Douglas, M., *Purity and Danger*, Routledge & Kegan Paul, London, 1966.

Ehrenreich, B., and English, D., *For Her Own Good*, Anchor Press, New York, 1978.

Eichenbaum, L., and Orbach, S., *Understanding Women*, Penguin, Harmondsworth, 1983.

Ernst, S., and Goodison, L., *In Our Own Hands*, The Women's Press, London, 1981.

Ernst, S., and Maguire, M., *Living with the Sphinx*, The Women's Press, London, 1987.

Fairbairn, W. R. D., *Psychoanalytic Studies of the Personality*, Routledge & Kegan Paul, London, 1952.

Flax, J., 'The Conflict Between Nurturance and Autonomy in Mother-Daughter Relationships and Within Feminism', in Howell, E., and Bayes, M. (eds), *Women and Mental Health*, Basic Books, New York, 1981.

Graham, H., *Women, Health and the Family*, Harvester Press, Brighton, 1984.

Guntrip, H., *Schizoid Phenomena, Object Relations and the Self*, The Hogarth Press, London, 1968.

Klein, M., 'Love, Guilt and Reparation', in Klein, M., and Riviere, J. (eds), *Love, Hate and Reparation*, The Hogarth Press, London, 1937.

Klein, M., *Envy and Gratitude and Other Works*, The Hogarth Press, London, 1975.

Kohon, G. (ed), *The British School of Psychoanalysis. The Independent Tradition*, Free Association Books, London, 1986.

Lawrence, M., 'Anorexia Nervosa: The Control Paradox', *Women's Studies International Quarterly*, 1979, vol 2, 93–101.

Lawrence, M., 'Anorexia Nervosa: The Counsellor's Role', *British Journal of Guidance and Counselling*, 1981, 9, 74–85.

Lawrence, M., 'Education and Identity: Thoughts on the Social Origins of Anorexia', *Women's Studies International Forum*, 1984, vol 7, no 4, 201–9.

Lawrence, M., *The Anorexic Experience*, The Women's Press, London, 1984.

Lawrence, M. (ed), *Fed Up and Hungry*, The Women's Press, London, 1987.

Lawrence, M., 'Anorexia and Bulimia: A Psychotherapeutic Approach', *British Review of Bulimia and Anorexia Nervosa*, 1987, vol 1, no 2.

Macleod, S., *The Art of Starvation*, Virago, London, 1981.

Mitchell, J., *The Selected Melanie Klein*, Penguin, Harmondsworth, 1986.

Orbach, S., *Fat Is a Feminist Issue*, Hamlyn, London, 1979.

Orbach, S., *Fat Is a Feminist Issue 2*, Hamlyn, London, 1984.

Orbach, S., *Hunger Strike*, Faber, London, 1986.

Orbach, S., and Eichenbaum, L., *Bittersweet*, Century Hutchinson, London, 1987.

Palmer, R. L., *Anorexia Nervosa*, Penguin, Harmondsworth, 1980.

Roche, L., *Glutton For Punishment*, Pan, London, 1984.

Roth, G., *Feeding the Hungry Heart*, Grafton Books, London, 1986.

Roth, G., *Breaking Free*, Grafton Books, London, 1984.

Showalter, E., *The Female Malady. Women, Madness and English Culture, 1830–1980*, Virago, London, 1987.

Winnicott, D. W., *Through Paediatrics to Psychoanalysis*, The Hogarth Press, London, 1975.

Winnicott, D. W., *The Maturational Processes and the Facilitating Environment*, The Hogarth Press, London, 1965.

Winnicott, D. W., *Playing and Reality*, Tavistock, London, 1971.

Woodman, M., *The Owl Was a Baker's Daughter. Obesity, Anorexia Nervosa and the Repressed Feminine*, Inter-city Books, Canada, 1980.

INDEX

—